Lasting Love . . .

How It's Found

Also by Debbie J. Papay

Blooper Episodes in Estate Planning and Elder Law:
Lessons From Prime Time TV
(Olive Grove Press, 2012-2013)

Contributing Author,
Love, Money, Control: Reinventing
Estate Planning
(Quantum Press, LLC, 2004)

Contributing Author,
Strictly Business: Planning Strategies for
Privately Owned Businesses
(Quantum Press, LLC, 2002)

Lasting Love . . .

How It's Found

Volume I

True Tales As Told To

Debbie J. Papay, Attorney

Olive Grove Press, LLC
Maumee, Ohio

Publisher: Olive Grove Press, LLC
                                  www.OliveGrovePress.com
Cover Design: Mary Ross Creative Design
Front Cover Photographs:
    Romantic Couple: © Jduggan / Dreamstime.com
    Vintage Compass: © Creativeye99 / Dreamstime.com
Interior Illustrations: See Appendix
Rear Cover Photographs: JLK Photography
                                  www.jlkphoto.com

Printed in the USA

ISBN: 978-0-9882695-5-2

Library of Congress Control Number: 2014900606

BISAC Codes:

FAM055000, FAMILY & RELATIONSHIPS/Marriage & Long
           Term Relationships
FAM029000, FAMILY & RELATIONSHIPS/Love & Romance
LAW035000, LAW/Estates & Trusts
LAW090000, LAW/Wills
LAW107000, LAW/Elder Law

This publication is designed to provide accurate and authoritative information in regard to the subject matter covered. It is provided with the understanding that neither the publisher nor the author is engaged herein in rendering marital counseling or matchmaking, or legal, accounting, or other professional services. If legal advice or other expert assistance is required, the services of a competent, licensed, experienced professional should be sought in person.

Dedication

With perfect timing, Henny Youngman (1906-1998) said "Take my wife, . . . please!" and the audience roared, even the married couples! For while they knew the joys and comforts of having a lifelong best friend, they also knew all too well the shock of finding out how frustrating the new "roommate" can be at times. From toothpaste caps, to toilet seats, to TV remote controls; from eating, sleeping, dressing, driving and housekeeping habits, to how money is spent and children and pets are raised; from stands on religion and politics, to involvement in sports and hobbies—it all takes adjustment and compromise to intertwine two adult lives 365 days a year.

This book is dedicated to the married couples everywhere who made it through their challenges together for decades, with humor, grace and mutual respect and commitment. It is especially dedicated to those who lived through World War II and created the ensuing economic, industrial and technological booms. Thank you for protecting and building our country.

> Debbie J. Papay, Ohio licensed
> and VA Accredited Attorney
> Bayer, Papay & Steiner Co., LPA
> Maumee, Ohio
> November 11, 2013
> Veterans Day

Preface

"The LORD God said, 'It is not good for the man to be alone. I will make a companion for him who corresponds to him.'"

> Genesis 2:18
> The NET Bible ®, New English Translation, Copyright © 1996-2006 by Biblical Studies Press, LLC, http://netbible.com All rights reserved.

"Whoso findeth a wife findeth a good thing, and obtaineth favour of the LORD."

> Proverbs 18:22
> The Holy Bible, King James Version.
> New York: Oxford Edition: 1769;
> King James Bible Online, 2008
> http://www.kingjamesbibleonline.org/

Jerry: "You complete me."
Dorothy: "You had me at 'hello.'"

Jerry Maguire (played by Tom Cruise) and Dorothy Boyd Maguire (played by Renee Zellweger), in the movie "Jerry Maguire"

Introduction

There are over seven billion people in the world today. With that many people, how can someone possibly find his or her one, true love? The couples in this book often found their special someone when they least expected it. They weren't necessarily out looking for someone at the moment. They just opened their eyes, their minds, and their hearts to a person within thirty feet of them. They let a spark turn into a flame. Then they nurtured that flame. All these couples somehow managed to find their soul mate in the first place, and then maintain that relationship for 25, 35, . . . sometimes 65 years or more. This compilation of stories of how couples found their true love is intended as a tribute to them—a way to pass on their story and legacy to future generations—and a ray of hope for those who have not yet found their "one."

At this point you might ask, "Why is an estate planning attorney assembling 'how we met' stories?" You might not realize that love plays a very central role in estate planning. When you love someone, no matter what kind of relationship it is (grandparent/grandchild, husband/wife, sibling/sibling, parent/child, etc.), you should want to do at least two things from a legal standpoint:

First, you should want to ease your loved one's burden in taking care of <u>you</u> when you suffer a period of illness or disability. It is similar to what the airline attendants tell you: "Put <u>your</u> oxygen mask on first." That instruction has to be said because it is often contrary to our protective instinct to first reach out to help the elder or child seated next to us. Those flight attendants know what they are talking about. If <u>you</u> become unconscious, you can't help your loved one. You <u>have</u> to take care of yourself first in some situations, for your companion's sake. Therefore, responsible, loving people come to estate planners for their oxygen masks: powers of attorney for health care and finances, revocable and irrevocable trusts, disability instructions, HIPAA waivers, asset protection plans, and other tools to make helping them easier for their loved ones.

Second, when you have loved ones, you should want to ease their burden in handling your affairs after your death. Your departure is going to cause them great emotional pain. That pain may result in physical ailments as well (sleeplessness, loss of appetite, indigestion, headaches, physical repercussions of stress, etc.). Your illness or passing may cause your loved ones some economic burdens (lost shared income and benefits, time taken off work, travel expenses, baby-sitters, and more). Why make this worse by failing to plan to prevent additional burdens—the easily avoidable complications in the legal, accounting and financial worlds? If you fail to plan, you have actually *planned* for the failure of your loved ones and the situation in which you left them. For example, consider the 25 year old killed in a car accident and having no Will. His parents have to spend their own money to post a bond and ask permission to handle his probate case. That was easily avoided by a simple Will plan. Consider the 55 year old dead of a heart attack with no planning in place. He was buried when he really wanted cremation, and some life insurance no one knew about went to the state's unclaimed funds department. Consider the deceased 85 year old with a Will but lacking a trust. The family paid unnecessary court costs, estate taxes and attorney fees, and subjected their family matters to unnecessary delays and the public eye. Again, this was avoidable with proper planning. *When you love someone, shouldn't you take better care of them than that, by planning ahead for what they inevitably will have to go through with you?*

Thus love and loving relationships, especially those of married couples, are key motivators to get legal estate planning documents in place initially, and to get them regularly maintained through the years.

Estate planning is a very personal area of law. Attorneys who choose that specialty usually love to talk to clients about their lives, their hopes and dreams for their beneficiaries, and their own legacies. "Do you mind telling me how you two met?" is my absolute favorite question, one I started asking clients three decades ago. How I wish that I had written down all the sweet, funny and amazing stories I've been told.

Love, relationships and marriage have been written about since mankind could write, or even draw on cave walls. The relationships are memorialized from the Bible to the Beatles to the Backstreet Boys; in poetry and prose; in stage plays, operas, symphonies, movies, songs, television shows, novels, self-help books, text books, comic strips, painting, sculpture, photography and more. What could possibly be added? No attempt will be made here. What follows, with great respect and warmth for every couple, are just their true success stories from real life and their words of wisdom for future generations. The experience of these 42 couples spans over 1,970 years of marriage, for an average of 47 years each. We should heed their advice in their "Secrets for Success!"

Please enjoy these stories. As you do, please consider including parts of *your* story – *your legacy* – a little of your *essence* – in your written, legal estate and disability plan!

Table of Contents

Dedication

Preface

Introduction

How Lasting Love Was Found, True Tales, in chronological order by the year the couple "met":

Stanley & Ruth, as told by Lynda

Stanley and Ruth met while attending the same one-room school house. That statement seems simple, but it really is the tip of an iceberg for a lifestyle we can't even imagine by today's standards.

You have to understand the times they lived in. Stanley and Ruth were both born in 1910, and we think they met in school between 1916 and 1924. Back then, there were no school buses. The "new" Ford Model A automobile hadn't even been produced yet. Very few people had a car. Children walked to school, or got a ride on a horse or wagon if they were lucky. That meant there had to be a lot of small schools everywhere. Schools were not large centralized buildings. These schools were much like you may have seen on the television show "Little House on the Prairie." They were literally a one room building. There may have been a partition near the back entrance to keep cold air from pouring directly in as each student entered, but otherwise you walked in the door and you were in the classroom, the only classroom. Maybe there were some coat hooks and benches to take your boots off. There definitely were windows (no air conditioning) and one wood stove to heat the whole place. There were a desk and black chalkboard up front for the teacher. Oh, and a prominently displayed paddle or switch. Each student's family had to contribute a load of firewood to the school for the winter and take turns with maintenance of the unisex outhouse. There might have been a hand pump water spigot out in the yard. That's about it. Students of all ages, first grade through high school seniors (if they were allowed to go to school that long), sat in the same room, within eye sight and ear shot of each other. One teacher taught all ages, and all subjects. While she was working with one group, everyone else was quiet. Or else. You brought your lunch—maybe a potato you'd put on the stove when you arrived so that it would bake through by noon.

The other children at the school lived in the same rural area. Their houses were often heated by coal, and the cooking stove in the kitchen burned wood—and your arms. Light was provided by coal oil (kerosene) lamps. We were told that "when electricity came down the road," Ruth's parents were so overjoyed to get electric lighting that they took their glass lamps outside and threw them against the stone foundation of the barn to break them and empty out the fuel.

Being able to eat regularly took planning and work, not shopping. Most families kept a dairy cow or some goats for milk and butter, and a few chickens for eggs and meat. Almost every household had a gun, a fishing pole, and someone who used them to bring home some meat: squirrel, duck, pheasant, quail, rabbit, geese, turkey, deer, fish or turtle. They planted apple, peach and pear trees, some blueberry and raspberry bushes, and maybe a walnut tree. Some families raised a few pigs, lambs or cows to butcher. Everybody had a garden for vegetables and canned what they could. Grandparents often lived in your house with you and your parents. Everything was shared, always. At one point Ruth's mother baked 14 loaves of bread every other day, including some for the motherless neighbor children who brought her flour to make bread for their household.

So imagine that was the world that Ruth and Stanley lived in as children. Ruth probably went to this particular school from ages 6 to 18, or from 1916 to 1928. Imagine being in the same school room for 12 years, possibly with the same teacher. Ruth walked the three-quarters of a mile from her house to the school, often with her brother, Philip. On the way there, they would pass the house of their Aunt Louise and Uncle Will Wagner. The Wagners had two daughters, Thelma and Jean, who also attended that school. (Years later, Ruth's cousin, Jean, became a teacher and came back to teach at her childhood school, teaching Ruth's little sister, who was 14 years younger.) Sometime during those years, Stanley came to live with the Wagners. He and Ruth became acquainted at school. Stanley waited for Ruth on weekday mornings and walked the rest of the way with her. Their school was at the corner of West Ridge and Russia Roads in Carlisle Township, Ohio, and it was built in 1886 (or earlier). It was red brick and it still stands today, now used as a residence.

Why did Stanley, as a child, come to live with the Wagners, people who were strangers to him? Stanley's father was brought to Berea, Ohio, from Poland to work in the Berea sandstone quarries. Later his wife, Mary, joined him. The couple had five children. All of them were very young when Stanley's father died of stone dust in his lungs, similar to what can happen to coal miners. Mary could not speak English and had few ways to support the children. Somehow a connection with Uncle Will was made. He had no boys, so Stanley, as a young child, was sent to live with the Wagners as their hired hand. For his bed and meals, Stanley was expected to work on the farm. As Stanley grew older, he had to leave school to earn money to support his mother and one sister (his other siblings having been sent to a children's home).

Even though they were no longer in school together, Stanley and Ruth kept in touch. On August 11, 1933, when they were both age 23, the couple eloped to Erie, Pennsylvania. At the time of their marriage, Stanley worked at the Harshaw Chemical Company, and Ruth worked as a nurse's aide at the Crippled Children's Home. They set up housekeeping in a huge, old home in Elyria that had been divided into apartments. (Coincidentally, this building later became a furniture store, where I worked for 20 years. I often ate lunch at work in the remodeled room that used to be my parents' bedroom!)

Ruth's father gave Ruth and both of his other two children separate parcels of land on the same road as his farm. Their father was a cabinet maker. As each child became able financially, he helped them build their homes. He told them to save up $500, and then they would start. So they built $500 worth of house. By then Stanley would have a little more money saved, and they would build a little more house. It was "pay as you go"— no mortgages. Remember, this was still during the Great Depression. Debt was viewed as a source of ruin. Ruth budgeted by the envelope method. She kept envelopes labeled Auto, Insurance, Taxes, Repairs, etc., and she would put a designated amount of cash in each envelope each payday. That way there was money ready in the envelope when the bill came due. Ruth's father was a cabinetmaker with the Amherst Lumber Company. He would bring home windows and other pieces of construction material for the couple in his Model T Ford. The project was a long haul, but the young couple was patient. Stanley and Ruth waited until their home was complete to have their two children, in 1942 and 1947, respectively, as well as a series of ponies and beloved dachshunds.

Stanley retired from Harshaw after many years of service. Ruth worked part-time, helping the neighbor lady with catering jobs, in an interior decorating studio as secretary, as a candy lady for Fanny Farmer, and finally, helping with estate liquidations preparation and selling. Stanley passed away in 1995, at almost 85, after 62 years of marriage. Ruth followed in 1996, pushing age 86. We have many fond memories of both of them and think of them and their lessons frequently.

Secrets for Success: You asked how they stayed married so long. I don't think they thought there was any other option. They were a product of their times. Hard work was all they knew all their lives, and once you made a commitment, you stuck with it, through thick and thin. You didn't just give up or back out when things became inconvenient.

Editor's Note*:* This story wound up being more about their lives and the times, than how Stanley and Ruth actually met and got married. We've included it as a tribute to the hardships their generation overcame and to offer historical perspective for the next dozen stories of couples who take us through Prohibition, World War II and the Korean War.

Clement & Celestine, as told by Clement,
supplemented by Sue

Celestine was her given name, but everyone called her Sally. Sally's parents died when she was young. She and her sister and two brothers went to live in an orphanage. When Sally turned 16, she checked herself out of the orphanage and took her three younger siblings with her, acting as their mother. To support them all, Sally got a job working as a waitress in a diner in Michigan near the Ohio border. This was before Michigan and Ohio ratified the 34th Amendment to end Prohibition in those states on April 10 and December 5, 1933, respectively. Sally soon realized the "diner" was actually a "speak easy." Occasionally she had to take a sandwich up to the man in the crow's nest who kept lookout with a machine gun!

7

A very popular activity back in those days was to go to the new dance hall on Madison Avenue in downtown Toledo, known as the Trianon, built in 1925. Here's how author Clint Mauk described it:

> *Then there was the Trianon Ballroom. Talk about finding romance and falling in love! A night of dancing on the 60 by 180-foot dance floor cost 25 cents. Patrons could find romance and fall in love to the sounds of the best bands in the land. Giant mirror balls cast a romantic shower of diamonds over everyone. Great entertainment came from the Dorsey Brothers, Benny Goodman, Glen Miller, and Toledo's own Helen O'Connell. So-called "low" beer, or 3.2 beer, nickel Cokes, and all this wonderful music made it so easy to fall in love at the Trianon. And if nothing else, more marriages were created at the Trianon than anything else. Good behavior was demanded and enforced. Acting up could result in being banned from the Trianon, sometimes for life! To many, this was the ultimate penalty.*

Sally loved to dance, and she danced with most of the young men who asked her. One night in 1937 a dashing young man, Clement, asked her to dance. They hit it off right away, and Sally let Clement walk her home that night. After that, Clement put out words of warning at the Trianon that managed to keep the other young men from asking Sally to dance. The two became exclusive. Clement's nickname was "Red," after his hair color. He called Sally "Sten."

---

*Mauk, Clint (3/24/09) "Entertainment: The Good and the Bad." Toledo.com. www.toledo.com/index.php?src=news&srctype=detail&category=inToledo&refno=143. Retrieved 11/11/2013. Used by permission of Mr. Mauk.

Clement was five years older than Sally, so they dated for quite a while by comparison for that time period. They were married in 1940 and rented a house in North Toledo. Then World War II unfolded. Clem joined the Navy in 1944. Sally and their three month old baby, Barbara, waited for his return from the South Pacific, and eventually the Okinawa Campaign. Clem knew what he was getting into when he joined the service. He was old enough to remember the time when he was about six years old, and he and his family went to the funeral for a neighbor boy who was killed in the First World War. Sally waited not only for her husband to come home from the war, but for her brothers: Norm, in the Merchant Marines, and Stanley, in the Marines.

Luckily Clem did return home. But by now Barbara was over two years old and her father was a stranger to her. It took a long time for her to accept him and come to him. Sally and Clem had their second child nine months after Clem came home—thus the phrase "Baby Boom!" Eventually they had four children total, and several beloved grandchildren and great grandchildren. Sally and Clem loved to travel, and did so in 49 of the United States, as well as in Europe. Sally died after 54 years of marriage. Clem missed her dearly until his passing just four months short of his 100th birthday.

Secrets for Success: Clem and Sally never talked about their secret to staying married for 54 years. However, they had several shared interests, like belonging to the American Legion and being very active in that organization. Clem was State Commander in 1979. Sally was active in the Ladies Auxiliary. They were on a mom and pop bowling team. They were strong family people, with Clem's mom living within walking distance and usually hosting Sunday and holiday dinners. Their children grew up knowing their cousins very well, seeing them most Sundays and all holidays. Family was first to Clem and Sally. That probably had a lot to do with their longevity as a couple.

John & Dolores, as told by John

Dolores, or Dee as we call her, was the younger sister of my friend, Jim. Dee and I must have first "met" around 1938-1940, while we were both in grade school. We were friends from that time through high school, but we never really dated. We were both born in Brooklyn, and our families later moved to Queens before we started school. All through school, to me she was just "Jim's little sister." In our neighborhood in Cambria Heights, Long Island, New York, we visited the same ice cream parlor, movie theater, park, church dances, etc., and we both attended the same church, Sacred Heart Parish. So we saw each other a lot.

While I was attending Hofstra College in Hempstead, Long Island, I had a route delivering eggs in order to make money. Dee's parents were good customers (two dozen eggs). I occasionally saw Dee on my deliveries, and we became good friends. But she was still the pig-tailed, freckled-faced "little sister" in my mind.

That all changed when I had my first furlough from the U.S. Air Force in 1951 and got to see her again. I was 21 and she was a year younger. My, oh my, how she had grown up in such a short time to become a beautiful young lady! We went out a few times, but then I had to go back and play airman for awhile. I had volunteered for service, and the Korean War was on. For the next furlough, I had it arranged before I got home that we would date. We saw each other a lot then. That was my last furlough, as I was going overseas to Germany for three years.

My folks and Dee took me back to the base in New Jersey for deployment. I was so in love with Dee. On the trip, we stopped at a bar in New York City. It was there that I asked Dee to marry me. But she said "no"! She was only 20 years old at the time and, apparently, she had things she wanted to accomplish. Dee also wanted to travel before settling down. That was January, 1952. My fellow airmen and I boarded our ship, the U.S.S. General W. G. Haan, and headed out for Bremerhaven, Germany.

I was disappointed in Dee's answer, but I had to accept her decision. The voyage across the Atlantic Ocean and living in a foreign country were all new and exciting to me, and my duties kept me busy. So the pain of Dee's rejection started to fade. Before long, though, I received a letter from Dee basically saying she had thought it over and, if I was still willing, she would love to marry me. To this day I claim Dee proposed to ME. I have proof because I kept the letter, even though she wanted it destroyed. At one point in the letter she said *"when you've got enough money to buy an engagement ring, I'm willing to accept one."* Later she added *"You've heard me say 'what is God's Will will be.' I believe we have His blessings now, and He is the only one to guide us through to our wedding day. Say many prayers, John, that this wonderful thing will be pleasing in His eyes. It certainly is in mine."* Dee hated mushy letters, so she lightened it all up with this: *"unless, of course, you met some German hot potato already."* I flew home from Germany at my expense. We got married and I flew back to duty. Dee followed later by sailing alone on the S.S. America. She got her wish to travel! Since I was not of proper rank for government housing, we lived frugally by sharing a home with a German couple, Herb and Ada, and their family. (To complete the loop, years later our daughter and her groom, on their honeymoon, visited Herb and Ada, and were warmly welcomed.)

Dee and I were married on September 13, 1952. We have been together for over 61 wonderful years, and counting.

Secrets for Success:

1. We were and are friends.

2. Dee's rule: never go to bed angry.

3. Three words Dee's brother taught John to use: "Yes, my love."

Joe & Rita, as told by Joe

It all started around 1940. Rita was about 14 and I was about 15. As I remember, on Saturday evenings we would go up to the IFFO Hall in Metamora, Ohio, to watch the older young folks dance. I loved to watch them, but felt I could not dance myself, as I just never had the opportunity to have anyone try to teach me. One Saturday night, I spotted this gorgeous young girl, 5' 9", dancing with this older guy, about age 25. (He was fat, but the most graceful person I had ever seen on the dance floor.) Her name was Rita. *I fell in love with her right then and there.* On Saturday evenings Rita's parents would come to town for their weekly shopping, and the girls were allowed to go to the dance for a little

14

while. I never did get the courage to talk to Rita at those dances.

Later, at wheat harvest time, I got a job on a farm owned by a man named Joe M. One of my duties was to haul water by truck from a nearby manmade lake. (In the winter we used to cut ice from that lake and store it in saw dust for delivery in summer to the local folks for their iceboxes.) The water I hauled was to be used to produce steam by the Baker steam engine that powered the huge Baker thrashing machine to separate wheat from the straw.

Back then farmers gathered in groups to help each other harvest their own crops in turns. The host farmer's family always provided a huge meal for the volunteers. As luck would have it, Monica, daughter of my boss, Joe M., hired Rita to help with preparing and serving the meal. After we ate, Monica saw Rita showing an interest in me. She forced Rita to haul the garbage out to near where I was resting under a big willow tree. That was the very first time we spoke to each other. Then it was back to work.

Shortly thereafter, the potatoes were ready to harvest, and again Rita and I were chosen to help. We horsed around in the field as young kids do, throwing potatoes at and chasing each other, until Rita had an accident and tore the seat out of the flimsy pants she was wearing. That was the end of the horseplay and we both went back to our respective homes.

I did not see Rita again until school started. She had graduated from the 10th grade at Caraghar, Ohio, now known as Assumption, and was entering her junior year at Metamora High School. I was starting my senior year there. My house was located right across the street from the school, which made me the envy of all the kids.

I was re-introduced to Rita. Since I could not dance, she offered to teach me. I would run home for a quick lunch and run back to school. The stage had a spot to dance with a nickelodeon for music. We would dance through the rest of the lunch hour.

In February, 1943, I was in my senior year of high school. World War II was in full swing. I had to register for the draft, and they called me up before I graduated. I asked for and received a deferment until graduation, which was May 19. I left for the service on June 1, 1943. Rita and I were in love and she swore she would wait for me until I got out of the Army. While I was gone, I often wondered if she really would wait for me. I had a one week leave six months later. Then I was shipped over to Hawaii, then Eniwetok, then Kwajalein, then ended up on Okinawa, until the Japanese surrendered in 1945.

In January, 1946, I arrived home to find Rita *had* waited. We decided to not wait any longer. So on March 2 we were married, and we started the most wonderful 61 years of my life, before I lost her in 2007. I still hold Rita very close to my heart, as no one will ever replace her. We raised seven children and now have ten grand-children and nine great-grandchildren. I'm reminded of that willow tree where we first spoke. I expect Rita's and my family tree to keep growing and blooming long after Rita and I are back together again.

Secrets for Success: We had a lot of financial struggles in our early years. When our first child was born, I was making 96 cents an hour in a factory, and we could not make ends meet. I changed jobs a few times, trying to make things better for us. But when our fifth child was born in October, 1958, we were really struggling. Just then, I finally got a break. I seized that opportunity and worked very hard. It paid off, and we made it. I think there is no one single thing that guarantees a long term relationship. I look back at what WE endured, in the early years and wonder "has anyone I know had that kind of beginning? I really think not." It all worked because we loved each other through all the ups and downs. You have to start with love. Then we respected each other, communicated, trusted each other, believed in each other. Together, we just never would allow ourselves to be defeated by outside forces or circumstances.

Fritz & Ruth, as told by Fred

We don't know for sure how they met for the very first time. We think it was at a dance hall. But I can tell you about one of their early dates. Fritz was serving in the Army Air Corps in Texas. Sometime in 1941, he completed his training and was en route to his new duty station in Burma. He rendezvoused with Ruth in New

York City. Ruth was working at General Industries in Elyria, Ohio, and she took a train from Cleveland to New York. One highlight of their time together was an evening at the Copa Cabana nightclub. We still have the Copa's menu Ruth saved from that night. On one side was a drawing of a woman in a Carmen Miranda fruit hat. The menu shows that a Budweiser cost 75 cents and a Seagram's was $1.20. For Ruth to save that menu for 70 years, we know it was a fun night for them. They both loved to dance. The music and sights must have been memorable.

Fritz and Ruth were married October 20, 1941, and raised three children. In later years, when Ruth became ill, Fritz took over the household and loyally cared for her until his passing, despite his own physical limitations caused by a stroke. They were married over 65 years.

Secrets for Success: Watching them, I would say that they worked hard, played hard, went to church, and did a lot of things together as a couple.

Bill & Ginny, as told by Christine & Debbie,
supplemented by Gilbert

Bill and Ginny grew up in the Great Depression, on opposite ends of town. They attended different grade and middle schools, before winding up at the same high school in Elyria, Ohio.

Bill was a football player, and Ginny had a crush on him. Bill worked after school retreading tires. His best friend Gaye, had a girl friend who worked with Ginny at the Kroger grocery store downtown. This was 1941, so Bill was glad to have gotten rid of his old 1917 automobile (so old that it had wooden wheels!) and be driving a 1931 Ford "Model A" coupe. It had no back seat, just a front seat, and a "rumble seat," which was a contraption where an exterior seat could fold down from the rear area that today we would call a trunk. From the name "rumble," you can imagine that this seat was not a comfortable ride to begin with, and then factor in that the rider is *outside* of the passenger compartment, exposed to the elements! One night Bill offered to give his friends a ride in his Model A, so Bill was in the driver's seat. Ginny, seeing the opportunity to get to know Bill better, jumped in and took the middle seat, and Gaye sat in the passenger seat with his girl on his lap. That was the first "date." After that Bill and Ginny dated for the rest of high school. By graduation, in June of 1942, they were a couple.

News of World War II was a part of daily life then. Shortly after graduation, Bill enlisted in the Marines and was sent to Parris Island, South Carolina, for training. At one point Ginny, together with Bill's mom, Mary, took a train from Ohio down to see Bill at camp for a visit. (Ginny told us she was impressed by the size of South Carolina cockroaches, able to carry a slice of bread up a vertical wall.) At age 18 and from a poor rural area, this was probably Ginny's first time on a train or away from home for this distance. We marvel that her parents even let her go! Bill's mother must have been considered a sufficient chaperone. After training, Bill, and thousands of other brave young men, packed "like sardines" into trains to San Francisco, where they shipped out for over three years of service on ships and islands in the South Pacific. Bill's service included the Okinawa Campaign. We still have his Marine knife, used to open too many cans of Spam, his un-punched April, 1944, beer card, and some of Ginny's gas and food ration stamps.

We know Bill and Ginny wrote to each other during the War, but we don't know what happened to those letters and V-mail. At one point Bill mailed Ginny a souvenir outfit from the South Pacific—a grass hula skirt, a sea shell necklace, and a coconut shell bra. Ginny mailed him back a photo of her shyly posing in it for him. We saw photos Bill mailed to Ginny and how the mail censors used scissors to cut off the scenery and any objects in the photo backgrounds. The censors even cut out portions of Bill's letters. After a while, Bill asked Ginny to marry him in every letter. Finally, on one letter, the censor wrote in the margin: "You better take him up on it, sister." (Imagine having a perfect stranger read and write comments on your personal mail and take a pair of scissors to your letters and photos!) In an attempt to make Ginny jealous and accept his proposal, Bill wrote about a young French girl on one of the islands who did laundry for the G.I.s. Apparently *that* did the trick.

Over the next three years, Bill was promoted to Sergeant, and Ginny was promoted to traveling Relief Manager for Kroger stores. Finally the War was over. Bill debarked in California in November, 1945, and sent this telegram: "Arrived Frisco today. Be home soon. Love, Bill." A frugal message when the charge for the telegram was based on the number of words used!

In the 1940s there were barriers for a Catholic to marry a Protestant. (Their parents weren't too keen on the match, and Bill's priest told him that if he married a Protestant, he could never set foot in a Catholic church again!) Also money spent on a wedding could be used for items made scarce due to wartime production—new tires, or a used refrigerator for their first apartment (and the required under-the-table "tip" to the landlord above the controlled rent amount to even GET an apartment). So Bill and Ginny eloped to Covington, Kentucky, where they were wed in June, 1946.

Bill and Ginny raised and educated two daughters and built two homes "by hand." They built their first house "payday to payday," buying as many boards or bricks as they could afford each time. Bill worked at his job days, and worked on the home construction nights and weekends. The process took over seven years. People drove by and stared at the structure. Some even stopped and knocked on neighbors' doors asking "did those people building that house next door to you die or something?"

Bill was Hungarian, Ginny was German, and Ginny was a good cook of both ethnic and American foods. The family ate well, often with fresh, frozen or home canned food from their own garden and fruit trees, or fish caught by Bill. Each of them was very talented and they shared hobbies or indulged the other's hobby. Among their interests were gardening, tree grafting, antiquing, prize level fishing, flower growing and arranging, sewing, cross stitch, needlepoint, embroidery, decorating, lathe and other woodworking, metal working, fish lure making, bonsai tree cultivation, glass and coin collecting, pinochle, crossword puzzles, Jeopardy, wine making, and bird watching! Marine sharpshooter Bill also kept a loaded .22 rifle by the back door in case his arch enemy, "Chuckie" (a woodchuck seemingly on steroids) set foot in his manicured garden again. The pair was always busy, busy, morning to night, except for short powernaps to refuel. No time for lollygagging!

Bill and Ginny were married for over 54 years before Ginny died in 2001. Bill visited her gravesite everyday to talk to her. Two years later, in his final illness, Bill told his eldest daughter that Ginny came to visit him in the nursing home. They may have been parted physically for a short time, but never in spirit.

Secrets for Success: Their youngest daughter conjectures that because Bill and Ginny came from financial struggles, and were separated by War for over three years, they worked hard *together* to build what they had and save for the future. The teamwork must have made them very close. The 1930s-40s taught them the values of the patience, honor, duty, commitment, courage, sacrifice and loyalty they both demonstrated, and the real costs when any of those traits are lacking.

Richard & Dorothy, as told by Richard,
supplemented by Tana

It must have been some time in 1944. I was on leave from the Marines, visiting Chicago. I saw this gorgeous red head, a Navy WAVE, walking on the opposite side of the street. She noticed me, too. She crossed the street, walked right up to me and said "you belong to me." At the time I was a Marine Corporal and she was a Navy Storekeeper 3rd Class. We were both enlisted.

After our leave was over, Dorothy had to go back to duty in Cleveland, and I went back to the Great Lakes to be transferred to the North Carolina engine overhaul plant. We wrote letters to each other back and forth. One time I got a 62 hour pass and drove to Cleveland from North Carolina and back just to see her. Needless to say, I was late getting back and got in trouble over that one. I didn't regret it, though.

We were married in my mother and stepfather's home in south Toledo on January 25, 1945, while we were still in service. Dorothy transferred, and we both continued our service in Cherry Point, North Carolina. I was a Machinist with the Marine Aviation Separation Unit One, MCAB. We liked the weather down there, but Dorothy complained that North Carolina had the biggest cockroaches she had ever seen. (Apparently more than one girl from the northern states noticed this!)

We were discharged from the service in June, 1946. My Marine pay was $69.30 a month at the time. We settled in south Toledo. I worked as a tool and die maker at Haughton Elevator (later known as Schindler Elevator) and stayed there for over 50 years. We adopted two boys and a girl, and together we were a family. Prior to adopting our children, Dorothy worked for a clothing retailer in downtown Toledo, who she also did some modeling for. She was a stay-at-home mom while our children were young and she was a wonderful cook and baker. After our children got older, Dorothy became the kitchen prep supervisor at the Harbor House Restaurant. We were married almost 49 years before she passed in December, 1993, at age 69. I've been over 20 years without her now, and I still miss her.

Secrets for Success: We took our marriage vows seriously, for better or worse, in sickness and in health. After my wife had a severe stroke at her brain stem, I visited her in the nursing home *every single day.* Put your spouse first.

Thomas & Patricia, as told by Thomas

During World War II, I was stationed in England with the Eighth Air Force. I was just 18 years old and we were flying bombing missions over Germany almost daily. In my Quonset hut home, I had a poster of Rita Hayworth posted on the wall. I thought she was really beautiful. Before each mission, I asked her to bring me back safely. And you know what? She did. VE Day, or Victory in Europe Day, came on May 8, 1945.

I was honorably discharged from the service later that year. I returned to my previous job at the Lima Tank Depot in Lima, Ohio. While working there, preparing Army tanks for storage, I noticed a young, pretty girl passing by every day at 10 a.m. and 2 p.m. I made up my mind to meet her.

One day I was waiting for this girl to come by. I asked her what her name was. She replied that she was Martha, from Spencerville. I asked her to stop by each day and maybe we could get to know each other. As time went on, we connected very well and started smooching behind the tank. I asked her if we could date and she agreed, saying her fiancé was still in the Navy and they were to be married when he was discharged.

One day Martha came to me and said, "I have bad news for you. My fiancé has returned and I can't see you anymore." I was stunned. She went on to say, "I have a beautiful sister, Patricia, who is 18 years old. She is in nurses' training at St. Rita's Hospital in Lima. I'll introduce you to her." She arranged for us to meet. When I saw Martha's sister for the first time, I was amazed at how much Patricia looked like Rita Hayworth in that poster back in England! *I knew at that moment, <u>this</u> was the girl for me.* Little did I know the troubles that lay ahead as a result of my decision.

Patricia and I started to date, mainly going to the movies, as she had to be back in the nurses' quarters by 10 p.m.

After several months, Pat told me that she couldn't see me anymore. I asked why. She explained that her father said that I was Catholic and Italian, and that she was not to have anything to do with me. Needless to say, I was furious. I never met the guy! How did he know anything about me? I asked Pat where he worked. I told her that I was going to see him and find out what kind of man this was who was so prejudiced based on religion and nationality.

The next morning I went to where Pat's father worked. Before I could say anything, he told me to "get the hell out." "How did he know me?" I wondered. I never met or saw this guy. I told him I came here to talk man-to-man, and I was not leaving until I found out what he had against Catholics and Italians. He said that wasn't it and told me, "The real reason is that you're a drunkard, gambler, and loafer." I almost laughed at these accusations, as I was working and couldn't afford to drink or gamble. I told him that I just came from fighting a war to protect stupid guys like him. I told him that there was a guy named Hitler who didn't like Jews. "You know what he did? He killed six million of them." I told him, "So maybe you should figure out a way to get rid of these people that you don't like." Needless to say, he was furious and ordered me out again. I told him that there was only one person who would not allow me to see Pat again, and that was her. Then I left, knowing that I just made him more of an enemy. I knew I had a fight on my hands.

I told Pat that we would sneak around to date. I found out later that on occasion her father had me followed.

There was a place where all the young folks hung out to dance and maybe have a beer. One night Pat and I went there early, as she had to be in by 10:00 p.m. About 9:45, Pat said we had better leave. As we left and were walking down the street to my car, I saw three men coming toward us. One of the men came running, grabbed Pat and dragged her to his car. I started to run after this guy. As I ran, I was grabbed by the two other men, who were bigger than I was, and one of them warned me not to see Pat again, "or else." I was stunned. There I was alone, wondering what to do next. The guy who grabbed Pat was her father, and the other two were his friends.

After several days, Pat and I got together again and resumed our dating, not knowing what was going to happen. Pat had a birthday coming up. I thought that it would be nice to buy her an engagement ring for the occasion. Her birthday would be December 7, 1947, and she would turn 19.

I went to Hodosko Jewelers in Lima. I knew the owner personally, as he was a Catholic from St. Rose Church. I went in the store and said, "John, I need an engagement ring. I only have $20 to put down on it and right now I don't have a job." I was enrolled in Miami University of Ohio under the G.I. Bill at the time. John pulled out a tray of rings and said, "Take your pick." I said, "John, didn't you hear me?" He repeated, "Take your pick." So I picked a ring and planned to give it to Pat later that evening.

On the way back to the nurses' home from the movies that night, as I was starting to pull over to the curb, Pat yelled out for me to keep going. She was frantic, and I asked, "What's the matter?" She replied that her dad was parked across the street. I drove around to the front of the hospital and we entered the nurses' home from the rear. Pat was crying and I made up my mind that this was it. I would go to where her father was parked and finally have a showdown. But when we got to the front door, I looked out and saw that his car was gone. That was probably a good thing. Who knows what would have happened?

So now the evening was ruined for giving Pat the ring the way I planned. I was really upset. As I pulled the ring out of my pocket, I said, "Here's an engagement ring and you have to make a choice. It's either me or your parents." She made her choice and accepted the ring.

Somehow Pat's dad found out. He kept pressuring her about it, as to where the ring was, and threatening her. I was disgusted over the way she was being treated. At the end of my first semester at Miami University, I discussed with Pat the idea of her leaving nurses' training and eloping to Kentucky with me to get married. She agreed. I told her I would go to Miami (in Oxford, Ohio, southwest of Dayton) and leave the school, come back to where she was housed, pick her up, and we'd go to Kentucky.

I checked out of college, and came back to the nurses' home to pick up Pat. But another nurse told me that her dad had pulled Pat out of nurses' training and taken her home. I was devastated. No girl, no job, no college. What do I do now? So I mulled around for about a week, not knowing what to do. One morning the phone rang. To my amazement, it was Pat. She explained that she had to promise her dad that she would not see me again so he would allow her to resume her training. She was calling from the nurses' home. I asked her to meet me at a nearby restaurant so we could discuss what we would do. We decided not to get married. We decided she should finish her training, and graduate in 1948, a year from this time. She would be 21 years of age then and out of the grip of her father.

Pat graduated, and we got married on January 9, 1949, a month after her 21st birthday. I asked her if she would get married in the Catholic Church. She said yes. I also discussed with her about raising our children Catholic. She said that would not be a problem. So we got married, and had a small reception. Naturally, none of her family attended. She was crying on her wedding day and we both felt very badly about it.

Pat became pregnant very soon. I was working and living at my mother's place. Pat found out that her mother was sick and in the hospital. So Pat said we had to go see her mom. When we entered her mother's hospital room, her dad got up and turned his chair around so his back was to us. He would not speak to us. This was on Friday.

Father's Day was coming on Sunday. On Saturday morning Pat said, "If you go downtown, buy something for my dad." I was furious that she would ask me this because of how he had treated us. But Pat said, "He's my dad. Please do this." I went downtown and purchased a shirt and tie and had it wrapped with a ribbon. That Saturday night when we went to visit her mom, her dad got up and turned his chair around again. I had that Father's Day gift box in my hand and I almost threw it at him. I felt his behavior was so stupid. We motioned to her mom about the present, set it down and left.

We returned on Sunday night, Father's Day. When we entered the room, Pat's dad didn't turn his back to us this time and he said, "Hi." I grudgingly answered back, "Hi." He asked if we had a garden, and I said "no." He said, "If you come to our place in Spencerville, I have a garden and you can have some veggies." I was shocked. What a turnaround! After we left the hospital, we both agreed that it must have been the Father's Day gift that softened her dad. After that, we visited them quite often. Nothing was ever said about the problem Pat's father had with my religion and nationality.

In 1952 I joined the State Highway Patrol and we moved to Findlay, Ohio. We had neighbors with a large family who were Catholic. Unbeknownst to me, the wife took Pat to meetings at church to discuss becoming Catholic. One day Pat told me that she was going to take Holy Communion and become a Catholic. It really caught me by surprise, but I was glad. She said she was going to invite her family to celebrate the occasion. I didn't think this was a good idea, knowing how they felt about Catholics. But Pat had the dinner and everything went well. For the first time I felt that all the turmoil that we suffered from when Pat and I met, hopefully, ceased to exist. At that point I thought, "I'm hoping we live happily from now on." We're in our 80's now. We've raised four good kids and have had 65 years of happy marriage.

Secrets for Success: Continuing love. Trust. Know each other well before marriage. No arguing about politics or religion. No excessive gambling or drinking. Mutual respect. Compromise on any differences. Take good care of your mate in cases of illness. Treat your spouse like you would like to be treated.

James & Carolyn, as told by Carolyn

My mother told me, "Church is the place to meet a boy friend." The only trouble was that this was the mid-1940s, and almost every available male was away in the military service in World War II. There were absolutely no fellows at First United Methodist Church, the small church we attended in Salem, Ohio.

As is the custom in the Methodist Church, ministers are moved around every seven or eight years. When a new minister arrived from Westerville, Ohio, his nephew, Jim, who lived in Toledo, began attending youth fellowship, as well as church. I wasn't the only girl at church who thought Jim was handsome. But I was the only one with whom he started walking home from youth fellowship each week.

In December, 1945, my high school football team was playing for the state title in a game in Canton, Ohio. Mauvareen, an older youth fellowship member, and her boyfriend were planning on driving to the game. Mauvareen offered to take Lois, my older cousin, and me. She suggested we ask a couple of fellows to go with us. I asked Jim if he was interested and whether he had an older friend he might bring along, thinking that could be someone for Lois. Imagine the looks on our faces when Jim showed up with his *age 50-something, married uncle, the minister!* Oh well, so much for THAT idea.

Jim and I had a great day during the drive to Canton and watching the game. We really, as you say, "hit it off." We look back after nearly 6 years of dating and over 63 years of marriage to December 1, 1945, which was our first date. Church, after all, was where it all began, and church still remains a central part of our lives together.

Secrets for Success: Marriage is a game of "give and take," but never try to keep score. Always be ready to forGIVE and TAKE away a lesson from each problem.

Ron & Harriet, as told by Harriet

It must have been near the end of 1945, because I know it was after both VE Day and VJ Day. After being at War for almost four years, victory brought a real boost to everyone's spirits. It wasn't just that we had won, but that it was *over*. The strain of it had been terrible. So even though millions of families had lost a loved one, generally moods were high with hopes of having a "normal" life again.

I was at Mike's Bar one night, at South and Spencer Streets in Toledo, Ohio, with my sister. She saw a boy she knew named Ron. He had served in the Army

Infantry in Europe during the War, but tonight he was in civilian clothes, as he had been recently discharged. My sister introduced me to him and we talked.

At some point Ron asked to borrow a dollar from me. On my dollar, we shared a cab to downtown Toledo, where we went to Kewpee's Hamburgers to eat, and then we shared a cab back home. Two people could do all that on one dollar back then! (You remember Kewpee's, don't you? Not spelled like the Kewpie dolls, but they had a picture of one on the sign? They were famous for flat buns and square burger patties, and their slogan: *"Hamburg, pickle on top, makes your heart go flippity-flop!"*)

I was 19 when we met, and Ron was 25 with a three year old son. We were married within six months, on June 1, 1946, in Trinity Lutheran Church. We've stayed married almost 68 years so far.

Secrets for Success: You asked me what the secret is to being married that long, and my answer is that you both just have to give. For example, Ron STILL has never paid me back that dollar he borrowed!

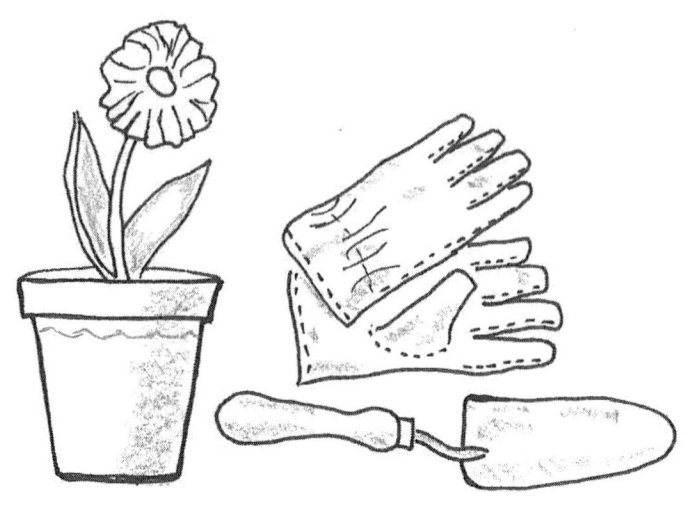

Jack & Eleanor, as told by Jack

In May, 1946, I was not yet working, having just been discharged from the Marines in April. One day I was driving down the street of our Ohio town with my friend, Bill. I had a light blue, 1939 Studebaker Champion that I bought as a used car from a Cadillac dealer. That was some "ride"! World War II was over. Things were hopping. It was a beautiful, early summer day, and we were *cruising*!

Bill spotted two girls walking along the street who he thought we should meet, so he urged me to turn the car around. I pulled into a driveway to do just that. My eyes fell on Eleanor Jean, there in the yard planting flowers with her mother. *For my part, it was love at first sight.*

Later I told my youngest sister, Donna, about this, and she said she knew Jean. Donna said that Jean was not dating anyone at the time. So Donna introduced us. Jean was not working either, as school had just let out for the summer. I asked Jean out, but she was not allowed to go to the movies. So for our first date we had to visit her aunt and uncle in Zanesville. For our second date, the next night, we had to go to church.

Two years later we were married in the Methodist Church in Moxahala, Ohio, on June 5, 1948. I was in strip mining for 40 years. Jean became a teacher and later a principal. We have been married over 65 years. We have two sons, four grandchildren, and four great-grandchildren. Jean has Alzheimer's now, but she can still read the Bible!

Secrets for Success: You asked our secret to staying happily married for so long. The secret is working *together*. If you have an argument, and you will, work it out. Don't walk away. Maybe you'll be as happy as we have been.

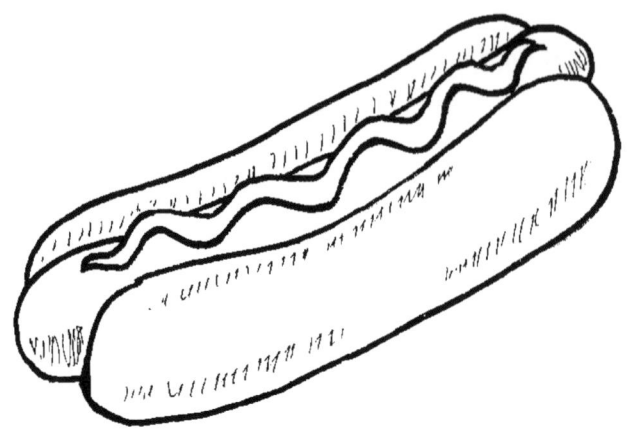

Daniel & Esther, as told by Janelle

Esther's best friend while growing up, and throughout her life until she recently died, was Ginny. Ginny had a boyfriend named Ed. Ginny and Ed hatched an idea. Ginny invited Esther to a wiener roast that Ed and Ginny were planning. Several other people would be there. One of them was Ed's best friend, Danny. This must have been in the warm months of 1946, and this took place in Toledo, Ohio.

At the wiener roast, Esther noticed another woman had eyes for Danny. Esther thought to herself "hmmm, that woman is trying to steal someone's man." Danny had just come home from the service in World War II. Esther had just stopped dating another man. Ed and Ginny thought Danny and Esther would be a good match. So this was all a "fix up." The two were introduced, and they talked at the party. Esther decided that she liked Danny.

The next day Esther's sister, Helen, asked how the party went. Esther told Helen that Danny said he was going to call her, but she wondered, like all women do, if he really would. Well, Danny did call!

Esther and Danny married on June 21, 1947, when Esther was age 22. They had five children, and many grandchildren and great grandchildren.

Ed and Ginny also married and remained good friends with Danny and Esther. They are now both gone, and Danny died in 2006, after almost 60 years of marriage. Esther still misses him every day.

Secrets for Success: Mom and Dad did everything together. We went to church as a family. We always visited our grandparents weekly as a family. We had a boat so we could fish or swim or just take a ride, always as a family. Dad helped Mom cook in later years. They shopped together. We never saw Mom and Dad argue or have harsh words. Everyone was loved and treated with respect, even if things were not going well.

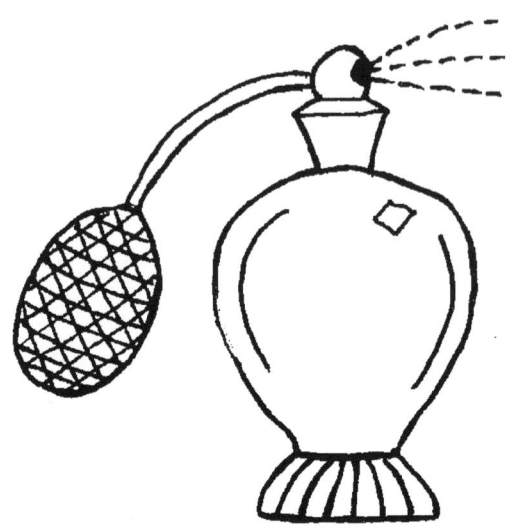

Gilbert & Barbara, as told by Gilbert

When I was in my senior year at Elyria High School (Elyria, Ohio), Barbara was a junior. So we were never in the same classes, but she really caught my eye when I would see her in the cafeteria at lunch time. She was shy, though. Sometimes I could get close enough to her that I could smell her perfume. It was intoxicating to me.

I signed up to work on the high school yearbook, called "The Elyrian." We were having a fundraiser where people donated their tax stamps. Barbara wound up in the same room as me, where our job was to tally up the stamps. Her girlfriend made Barbara come over to me and try to sell me some tickets to an upcoming hayride. Barbara shyly asked me if I would buy some tickets. I told her, "I'll buy some if you will go with me." That got her. This was in the fall, 1947.

I was really infatuated with Barbara on this hayride. But I couldn't even try to steal a kiss like I wanted to. There were two hay wagons, and a Pastor rode on ours. He was sitting back to back with me. It made me feel nervous and guilty just holding her hand in his presence. The night air was a little cold, so I offered Barbara a big red bandana that I had in my pocket. She used it like a scarf to cover her hair and she tied it under her chin.

The next day after the hayride, I had to help my dad dig around our septic tank. I kept pulling that red bandana out of my pocket and smelling it to get a whiff of Barb's perfume. I was so taken with that fragrance, and with Barb. My dad thought I was just gold bricking. He yelled at me to "put that thing away and get to work! Tie it to your nose if you have to!" I remember that my Aunt Laura Jean was at our house that day visiting. She really teased me about how smitten I was with Barbara.

At this time I was driving a 1931 Plymouth coupe that I had bought from Ginny, my oldest brother Bill's bride. I painted that car a bright blue, and I painted the spoke wheels bright yellow. I later found out that when I picked Barbara up for our second date, she looked out the window, saw my car, exclaimed "Oh my God!" and covered her face with her hands. Apparently she went out with me *despite* my car. That thing had a tarred cloth roof that leaked. When it rained, you had to use an umbrella inside the passenger compartment to keep dry.

One typical date for us would be going to the A&W for a ten cent root beer and a two bit hot dog. Barbara's mother was very strict with her, and she was a real tyrant about curfew. Barbara absolutely HAD to be home by 11:00 p.m. Sometimes we would have to walk out of a movie without seeing the ending, just so we could get her home in time. (Barb's mother even made her carry a big jar of Lady Esther Face Cream in her purse. The idea was that her purse would be nice and heavy, so she could swing it at any guy who got too fresh with her and the weight would do some real damage.)

I think back now about us a few years later. I was going to college at Ohio State University in Columbus. I used to hitchhike home to Elyria (up by Cleveland) and back on the weekends just to be able to see Barb. I couldn't leave Columbus until about 3:00 p.m. on Friday, and then I'd have to turn around and get back down there by Sunday night. It was worth it just to be with her a little while.

That brings us to the proposal. I was working at a surplus store in Elyria at the time. I told my boss, Marty, that I was going to propose to my sweetheart. He had just bought a brand new Buick convertible. It was yellow with a black top. Marty told Fred, another employee, to go wash and wax Marty's car so he could loan it to me for the proposal night! Then Marty asked me where I was buying the engagement ring. I told him, and Marty said the owner of that jewelry store was a friend of his. Marty said, "Let's go over and see him right now." So we did. The jeweler brought out the ring I had picked out to show us both, whereupon Marty insisted the jeweler only charge me wholesale. Then Marty suggested I give Barbara a "selection" of diamonds to choose from. The jeweler insisted I take the whole black tray of diamonds! Now imagine the position I'm in. I have borrowed a brand new car from my boss, and I have an entire jeweler's tray of diamonds to be responsible for. I am a nervous wreck. I was already petrified that Barbara would not say "yes." I decided not to give her a "selection," and I locked the black tray in the glove

44

compartment of Marty's car. I drove Barbara down to the back side of the Ford Road Bridge in Elyria. It was closed at the time due to damage from an accident, so the area was kind of a Lover's Lane. I knew I wouldn't be interrupted in my presentation. I proposed and Barbara said "yes." This was about July in 1951, and we were married in September.

Barbara and I were married for 62 wonderful years. She helped me at the office during the building years of my veterinary practice. Together we raised three beautiful daughters, and enjoyed three wonderful sons-in-law and four very special grandchildren. I still remember the smell of her perfume.

Secrets for Success:

1. Confess your love every day. Never, never go to bed at night, even if you had a spat or quarrel, without making up and maybe swallowing a little pride. End each day with a loving embrace and a kiss.

2. Get involved in your mate's interests, even if it is something that you don't particularly like. For instance, my wife really, *really* enjoyed shopping and would spend hours in a particular shopping center. I really, *really* hated shopping. But if you love someone, you accept the situation and roll with it. Barb would do the same for me. For example, Barb did not particularly like flying in our small plane. But she not only flew with me, she took flying lessons at my request to be able to land the plane in an emergency. Even with the fear she must have endured, I know she did it for the love we had. In simple terms, do not make your marriage one sided. Forget the "I, I, I" and think "we, we, we."

45

3. Praise your mate for the little things.

4. Do not forget birthdays, Valentine's Day and anniversaries. When I proposed to my wife, I asked if September 15 would be a good day to get married. She said yes, but she did not know my reason. I wanted that day because it was the opening day of hunting season and I knew I could remember that day for the next 100 years.

5. Of course, the standard flowers, candy and gifts on special occasions.

6. Last but not least, I think it really shows your love to your mate to renew your wedding vows at least once every 10 years of your marriage.

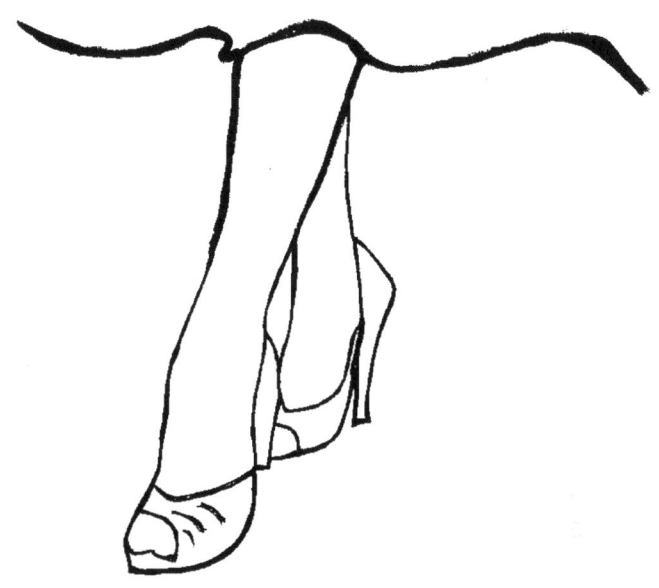

Thomas & Victoria, as told by Thomas

I attended an all boys' high school, Columbus Acquinas.
Victoria was a country girl. She had to ride a Greyhound
bus to her school, Holy Family, also in Columbus, Ohio.

After high school, I was a dyed-in-the-wool bachelor,
playing the field and working at the Columbus Dispatch,
where I ultimately worked for fifty years. Victoria was
shy and didn't date. She worked at the Bureau of Motor
Vehicles. We met at a Catholic Youth Organization
dance in 1950. When I looked across the room and saw
Victoria for the first time, *I thought she was the prettiest
girl I had ever seen,* and she had a great set of gams as
well! (I always was a "leg man.") We danced and talked
that night and then started to date. But I was drafted to

47

serve during the time of the Korean War. With me going off to face unknown peril, I told Victoria that I couldn't see any good coming out of us taking our relationship further at that point. I told her that I thought an awful lot of her, and if she was still here and available when and if I got back from military service, we could see what happened then.

So off I went. Victoria and I wrote letters back and forth to each other. She would make and ship me applesauce cakes packed in a box surrounded by popcorn all around. I mean real popcorn, not "Styrofoam peanuts."

At one point in the service I was in winter training in the mountains of Colorado. I was planning on coming home on leave for Christmas, 1951. I got a call that my father had died after shoveling snow. Ohio was locked in a record cold time period that year. I still have the letter he was writing to me the day he died. He wrote part of it, and then he wrote "I'm not feeling too well. I'm going to leave space here for Mom to add a note to you and go upstairs and lay down." He died in bed, presumably from a heart attack caused by exerting himself in that cold air. Dad had shoveled not only his driveway, but then he helped a neighbor. When I came home for my father's funeral, Victoria was waiting for me at my parents' house. I'll never forget that.

After I returned to service from my funeral leave, one of my assignments was on a joint mission with the Canadian military. We were sent to the Yukon Territory in 1952 for six months to test the effect of extreme cold on men and machinery. At times it was 50 degrees below zero. I was cold to the bone, lonely, grieving my dad, and homesick. I thought a lot about Victoria and the warmth of her smile.

We were married on July 25, 1953, in Victoria's country church. This past year was our 60th anniversary, and we are blessed to celebrate each other, our seven children, and our ten grandchildren. I look at Victoria and I still see that pretty, young girl I met at the CYO dance.

Secrets for Success: I was first attracted to my wife by her natural beauty, but I wanted to be sure that we shared the same dream of what a successful life should be. My father told me to look at your future wife's mother and you will find pretty much what your wife will be like. She was that—and then some! Victoria's family was so much like mine, even though she had siblings and I had none. I didn't know what love was—a natural attraction? a physical one? We just seem to think alike—it just plain feels good to be "with" her, whether we are physically together or apart at the moment. We were apart during my military service, for two years, and there was never anyone for me but her. After almost sixty-one years together, we are now separated by illness and I am lost without her. My advice: love each other. FAMILY IS EVERYTHING!

Ron & Sheila, as told by Ron

Sheila and I had the privilege of growing up in a small, conservative Indiana town of about 5,000 folks. Most everyone knew each other through school, church, work or community activities. All adults knew the kids in town and worked hard to protect, educate and nourish the young ones (even if they did not know the parents very well). I was two years older than Sheila, but since the town was so small, all students went through grades at the same schools. We first met through play-ground activities at recess in elementary school. Remember this was over sixty years ago, when many things were very different than today. As I reached the last year of elementary school and began to realize girls were different, one particular fourth grader seemed special.

She was not only cute, but she liked to play softball. That was about 1950.

As we moved on to junior high school, we decided it could be fun to meet at the local theatre for a cartoon and a movie and sit in the back row and giggle. I finally got up enough nerve to put my arm around Sheila during the movie and occasionally hold her hand. Our attraction continued through high school, where we both became band members and cheer leaders. It seemed like school activities kept bringing us together, not to mention that we only lived about three blocks from each other. My father had been Sheila's dad's teacher in high school, so each family knew the other as well.

As sometimes happens, I decided during my senior year of high school that perhaps there were other girls out there who were also worth dating. So we broke up for most of my senior year of high school. Sheila got even, though, by dating other guys. I went off to college at Indiana University in Bloomington, to experience life away from parents and small town living. During that year I began to realize that I missed the girl back home. I began to explore the possibility of getting back together with the one I had known for so long. Fortunately for me, Sheila also thought a connection was still there.

Sheila graduated and went on to begin her career as a secretary at a local company. I continued with college, which was 120 miles away from Sheila. The connection held, however, through irregular weekend visits home and holidays. Even though marriage was discussed, our parents thought that college was most important at that time, and that ages 20 and 18 were just too young to tie the knot. In Indiana at that time, men under age 21 could not marry without written parental permission, and my parents refused to grant permission!

At Christmas of my junior year, however, engagement seemed right. I proposed during my time home from college for the holiday and, fortunately, Sheila said "yes." Our parents finally realized that they each were soon to get a new daughter or son. I finally turned 21 during the summer between the junior and senior years of college. Sheila by then had been working and saving a few dollars, enough at least to buy a used Chevy. A wedding was planned for August before the start of my senior year of college. The wedding took place in the local church, as all weddings in that small town did, and the reception was held in the local community center of the town's largest employer, Owens-Illinois, Inc., where Sheila's dad worked his entire career. After the reception, we went to Florida for a quick and hopefully inexpensive honeymoon. After the honeymoon, we headed to Bloomington for my senior year of college. We needed a place to live and a job for Sheila.

With her secretarial training and experience, Sheila landed a job with Indiana University at the large salary of $225 per month. We found an apartment for married students just out of town at $100 per month. (This was in 1959.) I was able to complete my education while Sheila earned her PHT (Putting Hubby Through) Degree.

It was amazing that at 21 and 19 years of age we found a wonderful marriage with the one we had known for what seemed like forever. Stranger still was that after all those years, the connection between two kids in a small Indiana town held so strong, despite a breakup and all the new friends I met in college and she met at work.

After college, life changed. I began a new career, and a new baby came along for Christmas, 1960. Living in the Chicago area seemed a long way from the small town in Indiana where we both grew up. But that experience turned out to be a great learning time, and we grew stronger as our family grew. Now 54 years later we have experienced several career changes, multiple houses and locations for our careers, wonderful family experiences, unbelievable blessings and health, wonderful grandchildren and now our first great grandchildren. Life continues to exceed our every expectation in our 23rd year of retirement, with Florida and Ohio homes and many friends in both places.

Our lives show that locals from a small town can meet, experience life away from their parents, marry, survive the trials of marriage and family, and make it through all of the challenges all married couples face today. We have to acknowledge the influence our parents had on our lives and the support of so many wonderful people who we met and were influenced by as we progressed through all the stages of life. We look forward to many more years (hopefully) of more new friends and more life experiences.

Secrets for Success: I'm sure there are a thousand reasons why marriages do or do not work. Luck and hard work are always factors. In our case, we thought some regular rituals would help. Making sure that we expressed some daily commitment or re-affirmation of our choices of each other, we agreed that expressing our love to each other was important. We decided that every time we were not together due to work, errands, outings with others, etc., we left with a kiss three times. That, of course, meant "I love you." They were usually quick pecks as we were on our way out the door.

We also agreed that regardless of any marriage trials and tribulations, and arguments over what usually turned out to be trivial and ultimately unimportant differences of opinion, we should end the day with another re-affirmation. Although my wife goes to bed earlier than I do, she expects me to wake her before we both hit the hay for the night and end our day with this ritual we have now done for our 54 years together: I wake her up, kiss her on her forehead, nose, each cheek and chin, and we say to each other in unison: "I love you more than anything in the whole wide world, forever and ever and ever and ever and always, and then some, plus a whole lot." That ends our day together as we go to sleep. We have done this from the start of our marriage until today. I think that expression, confirmation and assurance wash away any negative things and make sure that we have those great feelings of having selected the right person and that our marriage is worthwhile. It seems to work and only takes a few minutes. Sometimes it seems lately that she does not often remember being awakened for our ritual but, rest assured, it happens.

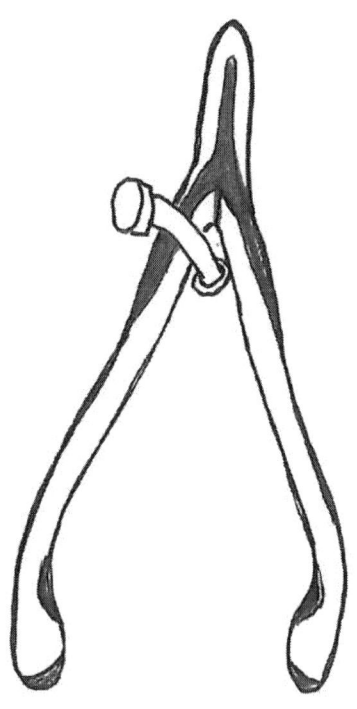

Jack & Ida, as told together

Jack said: "In 1952, my family moved to Sylvania Township, Ohio. We noticed that there were several young people congregating at the house kitty-corner from our new home. My mother suggested I may as well go over there, so I could meet the neighborhood kids all at once. I was 16 at the time."

Ida continued: "Our family had just had a whole turkey dinner. That day my brother hung the wishbone above the front door and said to me, 'You're gonna marry the next guy who walks through that door.' That next guy was Jack. I was just 15 years old."

Both: As our friendship developed, occasionally Jack would whistle at Ida from his driveway or the street. Ida's mother would yell out the door or window at him, "What'd you do? Lose your dog?" Sometimes when Jack would be over visiting Ida in the evening, Ida's mother would get out an alarm clock and start to wind it in our presence. That was her not-so-subtle signal that it was time for Jack to go home!

Our first official date was a movie in a theater. Occasionally we would also go to drive-in movies. Ida's sister would go along, and Jack would hide in the trunk on the way in through the ticket gate. Jack's best friend came to visit one time, and Ida's sister wound up marrying him.

We got married when Jack was age 20 and Ida was age 18. We have been married 57 years, and counting. When we have a whole turkey, we never waste the wishbone!

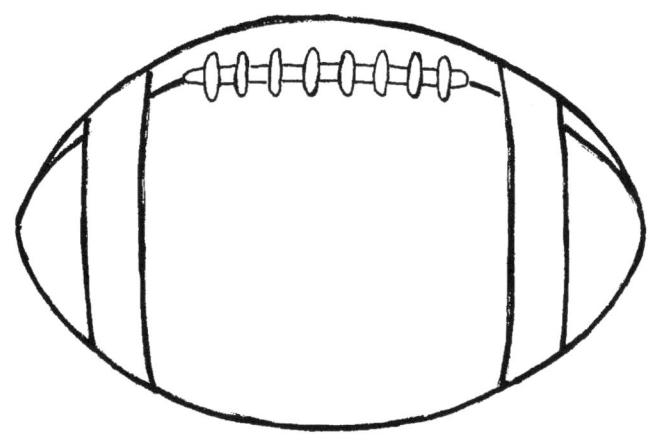

Gerald & Katharine, as told by Katharine

As children, Gerald and I attended the same church, St. Rose Parish of Perrysburg, Ohio, although we never really met. He went to Perrysburg High School, and I attended Troy-Luckey High School. Gerald saw me going to communion and thought "I would like to meet that girl."

Gerald saw me sitting with my mother, grandfather and grandmother every Sunday. He figured out who my grandparents were and where they lived. One day he went to my grandmother's house, knocked on the door, and asked if her daughter lived there. (He could be bold when he put his mind to it.) My grandmother told him "My daughter is married and has four children. You must be looking for my granddaughter." She then told him where I lived. After he left, she went to the telephone and called me to let me know he was on his way.

Gerald came to our house and knocked, and I answered the door. He introduced himself and asked if I would like to go on a double date with him to a football game that coming Friday. The other couple was his neighbor boy and the neighbor's girlfriend. I agreed to go. When I told the rest of my household, my father asked "Is he one of those crazy drivers?"

Gerald picked me up in a black Chevy coupe with whitewalls. He had bought this car from his brother, Norman, who was serving in the Korean War at the time. His mother had arranged this sale through the mail. I remember I was impressed with how Gerald had the car all cleaned up—it was "Spic and Span." This was October, 1952, and the football game we went to was Perrysburg vs. Rossford. Gerald was a junior in high school and I was in my senior year. I thought he was pretty cute. He wore a blue suede jacket and white buck shoes. It was popular in those days to park along country roads and do a little necking. If you were seen by somebody, everyone in school knew about it rather quickly!

After that we went to more football games, square dances, baseball games, and other activities. We continued to date, but we were "on again, off again," breaking up a few times like teenagers do. After we graduated from high school, Gerald worked for LOF (Libbey-Owens-Ford) in Rossford and was in the National Guard. I started out at the University of Toledo in medical technology, but then took a job working in the payroll department at LOF.

Gerald gave me an engagement ring around Thanksgiving, 1954. I remember my mother was a little surprised when I showed her. All she could say was "Well, you could have waited until Christmas!"

58

To be married in the Catholic Church, it was required that we first go through some counseling sessions with a priest. I remember Gerald and I were walking side-by-side following the monsignor at the parish house for one of these sessions. Gerald whispered something to me as we were walking. The monsignor, who was known for being very strict and who was called "Little Caesar" by many (he was about 5 feet tall), whirled around and told us sternly, "They'll be no secrets HERE!" He sufficiently impressed us with the seriousness of the proceedings.

We were married in May, 1955. We were both nineteen years old. We raised four wonderful children and had a great life together until Gerald passed in 2009, after 54 years of marriage.

Secrets for Success: What's the secret to a long relationship? Not being selfish! Also having respect for your spouse, being faithful and honest. Also not keeping any secrets from your spouse. For us strong Catholics, our faith helped us have a good marriage and helped us through the rough times. It's important to talk things out. Although we were young when we married, we knew how to accept responsibility. We weren't spoiled as children.

Jim & Connie, as told by Connie

On Christmas Eve, 1955, at the Misawa Air Force Base Officer's Club on Honshu Island, Japan, three recent transferees from Chitose and Ashya Air Bases sought the warmth of the fireplace to reminisce and celebrate—Jim, Jack and Camille. I was across the room, and a new arrival from Matsushima Air Base, listening to the orchestra play Christmas melodies. My friend, Camille, beckoned to me to join the officers in a toast to the holiday. As we four raised our glasses, little did we know that a new journey was beginning for me, a Department of Air Force Civilian from Toledo, Ohio, and Jim, an Air Force fighter and tactical support pilot for the North Pacific Theatre from Hackensack, New Jersey.

Jim and I found common interests and ideas during dinner dates and while meeting people in the surrounding towns we explored. Romance blossomed. We became engaged in front of another fireplace, this time in a small nightclub in the town of Misawa outside the base. As summer ended the following year, Jack was our Best Man and a dear friend, Cilda, was our Maid of Honor as we were married during a Catholic military ceremony at the Tokyo Chapel Center in Tokyo.

As newlyweds we were assigned to Mitchell Air Force Base, Long Island, New York, where Jim completed active duty service. Jim continued service in the Air Force Reserves and we moved to my home town, Toledo, where our lovely daughters, Stephanie and Dorian were born. Jim worked in management at National Laboratories, while my work with the Air Force continued nearby at Continental Aviation and Engineering. Later, Jim was asked by a former colleague to join the Administration at the University of Toledo, and I became a substitute teacher in the Toledo Public Schools. Because of my success in the classroom with deaf students, mothers of these students offered to help me become certified in this field. My career as a special education teacher began. We held these positions until our retirement.

Stephanie and Dorian followed us to become University of Toledo graduates. Their studies led Stephanie to law and to become a law partner, while Dorian chose education and teaching as her profession. Both daughters are married and have wonderful children who repeat their success.

It is an amazing story of over five decades for us, who began life together serving our country on the islands of Japan.

61

Secrets for Success: Jim's secret is compromise and then more compromise. My secret was found in nurturing and loving two beautiful daughters who woke up each day with new wonders that amazed and strengthened our marriage. Embracing brothers, sisters and other family members who enriched our lives added another dimension to a successful marriage. But the enduring secret is to love each other with kindness.

Lloyd & Donna, as told by Donna

Lloyd's parents' home and my parents' home were just one mile apart in Pemberville and Woodville, Ohio, both rural towns. We belonged to the same church. But there was an age difference between us, so we never really knew each other or spent time together.

Years passed. In 1956 Lloyd's sister, Carol, was getting married. Lloyd was in the Army at the time, but he came home for the wedding on a weekend pass. My brother's wife was in the wedding party. My brother was away in the Army, so I accompanied her to the wedding and I drove us. When Lloyd saw me at the reception, Lloyd didn't know who I was. He hadn't seen me since I was age 9. I had grown up and changed a lot during the 12 years he was away in the service! Someone told him who I was, and after that he came over to me and we talked quite a while.

Lloyd's brother was having a party at his home after the wedding reception. Lloyd asked me to go with him. I told him that I couldn't go, because I was supposed to drive my brother's wife home after the reception. She overheard me tell Lloyd that, so she offered to drive my car home so I could go with Lloyd, which I did. We talked more. Lloyd left the next afternoon to go back to camp.

Two weeks later, Lloyd came home on a two week leave. We dated all during his leave. By the time the two weeks were over, we had decided to marry. We set the date for the following April, 1957. Lloyd was 32 and I was 21. Between the time of his leave and our wedding date, Lloyd came home once a month to see me for a weekend. One month I drove to Granite City, Illinois, to see him. Every day we wrote letters to each other. I still have those letters. When we married, Lloyd had one more year to serve on that hitch. He told me he would quit the Army after that if I wanted him to do so. I wouldn't ask him to do that, so he re-upped for six more years. Then he retired from the Army and we moved back to Ohio to be near family and friends. We've been married for almost 57 years, and we raised three children together.

Secrets for Success: Only disagree about really important things. Don't waste time arguing about trivial matters. Help each other as often as possible.

Ken & Joice, as told by Ken

When I was a senior at Bowling Green State University (BGSU) in northwest Ohio, I saw all the photos on display of the candidates for the 1958 Homecoming Queen. There was one photo that really caught my eye. I thought the young lady was very, very attractive. A few days later I saw this same girl walking across campus! But I didn't know how I could meet her.

I soon graduated and entered the U.S. Army for a year of active duty. When I returned, I got my first teaching job in the Woodville School System. A faculty party was planned for Christmas, 1959. It was announced that two students from BGSU would be serving the teachers at the party. Mrs. Howard, the fifth grade teacher, had a daughter, Joice, who was one of the students serving punch. When I saw her at the party, I realized Joice was that same pretty homecoming queen candidate I saw on campus at BGSU a few years earlier.

After contemplating this evidence of destiny and fortifying myself with enough Christmas punch, I asked Joice for a date—for that same night! It was a Friday, so after the party, we went to a high school basketball game. Then we had two more dates right in a row. After the third date, Joice's father was really wondering what was going on. Back in those days there wasn't much open late at night in a small town, so we went to the turnpike plaza to get a Coke or a cup of coffee.

Before Christmas break ended and Joice was going back to college, I asked her to go steady. That meant that I had to pin her with my fraternity pin, but I didn't have one. So I borrowed one from a fraternity brother and pinned her. I never did buy a fraternity pin. They cost $60, which was a lot of money back then. Just recently I ran into a fraternity brother and he asked me if I ever bought a pin. Apparently I'm still known as a "cheapskate" for *that* one over five decades later!

We were married in June, 1961. That summer we started attending Grace Methodist Church in Perrysburg, where we are still members and have participated in many activities over the years. Our two children were raised in that church.

Some time ago, "our" turnpike plaza was scheduled to be torn down. On our wedding anniversary that year we went back to visit it one last time.

We just celebrated our 52nd wedding anniversary this past June.

Secrets for Success: Our faith and our church made an important, positive contribution to our marriage.

Make sure you choose wisely the first time and don't even date anyone you wouldn't consider marrying. You want to be with someone who shares the same goals and makes you happy, someone of whom you can be very proud to say "she's my wife."

Friends of ours, now married over 30 years, made a pact when they got married to never wear pajamas. Maybe that helps.

My brother has been married 65 years, and he always says "never go to sleep angry." I asked him if that works. He said "yes, but one time I didn't sleep for a week."

Another friend of mine said the secret to a long marriage is to take your wife to Hawaii for your 25th anniversary. Then for your 50th, go back and get her!

Joe & Dorothea, as told by Dorothea

I was born in West Virginia in 1926. I went to college and became a teacher and later the principal of a three room school. After my parents died, unbeknownst to me, my relatives in Ohio and Pennsylvania sent out applications for teaching positions in and around their towns, so I could move and be closer to them. As a result of that, I decided to try a job in Toledo, Ohio, and moved there in 1960.

I was in Toledo just six weeks when another teacher approached me and said she had someone she wanted me to meet. She suggested we could go to the Omega dance together. I wasn't keen on being fixed up, but I finally relented. So Joe and I met for lunch at a diner. I wasn't too sure about him. He seemed nice enough, but he was full of jive. He asked me to the Omega dance. I agreed with some hesitation in the back of my mind.

We dated for eight years. Then we were married for 38 years, before Joe died on Christmas Eve, 2006.

Joe was a good husband. We never had any problems— except just once. Shortly after we returned home from our honeymoon, I bought a decorative tree for inside our house. When Joe came home from work, he didn't comment on it. Then he didn't comment the next day either. Finally I asked him if he liked the tree, and he asked "who told you to buy that?" I let him know right then and there that I was a working, independent woman who got herself up out of bed every day and went to work, and I didn't need his permission to buy anything! I told him that if he ever questioned me again, I'd kick him out. After that, we never had another problem.

Joe was a good husband, and I miss him every day.

Secrets for Success: The Editor suggests that based on Dorothea's story, one of their secrets might have been mutual respect for each other's boundaries, or perhaps agreement on how marital finances should be handled. She also wants to say that when Dorothea spoke of Joe, she got a real twinkle in her eye! It made her wish she had met the man who was so full of "jive."

Phil & Kay, as told by Kay

Our story is kind of unique. We probably first "met" in 1939, shortly after I was born and Phil was only age two! Phil and I have known each other all of our lives. But we didn't start dating until 1960. Here's how that went:

My Dad and Phil's Mom lived across the street from each other in Blissfield, Michigan, as youngsters. My Dad introduced Phil's Mom to Phil's Father and they married in June, 1927. My parents married two years later in June, 1929. Phil was born in 1937, and I came along in 1939. We had lots of visits and playing time while we were growing up until about ages 12 and 10. Then our two sets of parents had a falling out. We never knew what the problem was.

Phil went into the Army in 1956 and was engaged to his high school sweetheart. While he was in Germany, he received a letter from his girlfriend stating that she and her family were moving to California. Well, the engagement was broken.

Phil came out of the Army in 1959. For some reason, his Mom called my Mom and we went to their house for dinner. I think his Mom was trying to get us together. Phil didn't pay much attention to me, and shortly after he became engaged again. Then there was another broken engagement. So a whole year passed.

Then my Mom invited Phil's parents over for dinner. Phil came along. That evening he was much nicer to me. We went for a ride and he asked if I would go out with him. I said "sure." Well he didn't call me until Friday of the next week, so I thought he was calling every other girl and only called me as a last resort. I almost didn't accept his invitation to go to a movie, but I am sure glad I did. That was in August, 1960, that we began dating, and in October he asked me to marry him. We were engaged on Christmas, and we were married in July, 1961. That was 52 years ago. I guess for Phil, the third time was the charm as far as engagements go.

I thank God for Phil every day of my life, as I could not have had a better husband.

Secrets for Success: Phil and I have always been believers in God and have always gone to church together and raised our girls in a Christian home. We have always tried to treat each other with respect, dignity and love. If we had a disagreement, or maybe it could be called a spat, when it was over, we always told each other we were sorry and that we loved each other. Also we never left the house or went to bed angry with each other. A lot of things that come up should be overlooked. Never feel a marriage should be 50/50, because that isn't the way it works. Sometimes it is 90/10. We've learned through the years that most things we fussed about weren't worth fussing about. Most of the time, it is better to just let things go.

We believe that a God centered marriage is the best, and if you are faithful to Him, he will be faithful to you. It isn't always easy, but it can be done.

Lee & Marilynne, as told by Marilynne

My husband and I met on a blind date when we were both in college. I was a freshman student at Mercy Hospital School of Nursing, and Lee was in his junior year at the University of Toledo in the College of Education.

It was Leap Year Day, February 29, 1964. My plans for the evening were to go to a fraternity party with my friends. My roommate convinced me to instead double date with her and her boyfriend and his best friend. We went to a depressing black and white war movie, "The Victors," at the newly remodeled, vintage Pantheon Theater in downtown Toledo, and then for burgers afterward. Lee had dated several of my friends. They suggested talking about his new car and football, and it worked! (The "new" car turned out to be a 1954 Chevrolet that Lee purchased for $50 from a college buddy!) We didn't go out together again for three months, as I was seeing a guy from my hometown of Bay Village, Ohio. But then we went out again, and continued to date throughout college. The night before my graduation, on May 20, 1966, in the front seat of his car, Lee surprised me with an engagement ring. Only this time his car was a new, 1965 Chevrolet Chevelle convertible that he had purchased the year before.

We have been happily married for 46 years and we are still talking about football, as he has coached for 49 years. Besides our three grown children and five grandchildren, we have been part of so many lives of the young men my husband has taught on the football field. Our two sons coach. Our oldest is a successful high school head football coach and T-ball coach. Our youngest son is a head little league baseball coach. Our daughter was a trainer for the volleyball team in high school. Sports have been a huge part of our lives together with so many positive experiences.

My husband and I have shared so much together and he is truly my best friend. We share just about everything: our thoughts, troubles, and dessert, too! We supported each other as he returned to college for his Masters Degree in High School Administration when our children were young, and I completed my Masters Degree in Nursing and PhD in Health Education as a Grandma.

We enjoy travelling together for pleasure and presentations of my research study at National and International Nursing Conferences. If he can bring his golf clubs, it works!

Even after all these years, he never forgets a dozen red roses on Valentine's Day, out to dinner or maybe a long weekend in Toronto for our anniversary, and very special birthdays!

We have met so many wonderful couples over the years who we go out with for dinner and a movie, or with whom we travel and volunteer together. Those friends have been an inspiration to us, as our own parents have been.

Secrets for Success:

1. Never take each other for granted. It is so easy to get in a rut. Do things out of the ordinary, like candlelight dinners, a walk at Wildwood Park, fixing his favorite meal, or leaving "I Love You" notes by his shaving gear.

2. Communicate! Ask about each other's day. Say "thank you."

3. Enjoy fun competition together. Lee and I have stayed up until 3 a.m. just so he could win at Gin Rummy!

4. Talk over major financial decisions and agree before moving forward.

5. Give compliments to each other. Tell him his butt looks cute in those jeans.

6. Go to church together every Sunday.

Bill & Vicky, as told by Vicky

Bill graduated from a neighboring high school two years before me. He was good friends with a group of guys from my school, Anthony Wayne, in Whitehouse, Ohio. They all loved their cars and getting under the hoods to work on them. I knew of Bill because of his association with my friends.

During the last football game of the season of my senior year, my friend, Ruth, came to me during halftime and asked if I was staying for the dance afterward (called "a sock hop.") This was 1964. Of course I was! I wasn't missing a thing my senior year! Ruth asked if I had a way home and, if not, would I go with Bill so that she could go home with her boyfriend, Mike. Ruth said,

"Bill's a really nice guy, and I really want to go with Mike." Ruth had an overprotective father who did not want her dating any one guy more than a couple of times. Ruth's plan was that if I went with Bill and he drove, then when we went to Ruth's house, Bill could take her to the door and her dad wouldn't know she was really with Mike. (Are you following this?)

With some hesitation I agreed, because Ruth and I were good friends, and good friends would do that for each other—right? I remember it was a cold, cold night and many people left the game soon after halftime. I stayed for the dance—danced my feet off—lots of different guys and girls, too—all of us having a great time together. Finally, it was time for the last song. Bill strolled over and asked me to dance. That was a good idea, since he would be taking me home. As we danced this slow dance together, I could tell he'd had a beer. (Legal age was 18 then, and the "guys" had left the freezing game at halftime and gone to the local bar to warm up.) My thought as Bill and I were dancing was "What has Ruth talked me into?"

After the dance, the four of us went to Bill's car. He had a really nice car! There weren't any places to eat out our way. Everyone usually went to Reynolds Road in Toledo, and that's where we went to eat—the White Hut. We had great food. I was impressed by Bill's manners and the way he treated me. Then we took Ruth to her house, trading seats before we got there. Bill escorted Ruth to her door, as planned, while I stayed in the car with Mike. Then Bill took me home. He told me he'd enjoyed the evening and asked if he could see me again.

Needless to say, we continued to date throughout my senior year and during my first year at college. We became engaged during my sophomore year and got married in 1966 between my sophomore and junior years. My grades drastically improved after I got married!

Bill has been the "wind beneath my wings" for almost fifty years, supporting me in all areas of my life. I am truly blessed!

Secrets for Success:

1. Laugh together.

2. PRAY together . . . and OFTEN!

3. A great argument every once in a while is good, too.

Bob & Sue, as told by Sue

Bob and I were both students at the University of Toledo in northwest Ohio. Bob was a football player and a Big Man on Campus. His friends were trying to find a nice girl to fix him up with. A friend of his asked a friend of mine if she knew anyone for Bob. She thought of me.

Bob refused to go out on a blind date. He wanted to see what I looked like before he asked me out. (Our joke is that it was suggested we meet at the University Library, and Mr. Football Player responded, "There's a library?")

It was finally arranged that we would both attend a Campus Crusade for Christ meeting. This particular meeting was the 1966 Halloween party. Bob had no idea what I looked like, but I had seen his football picture in the campus paper. So I spotted him at the party and I had fun dodging him. Everyone wore name tags, and

79

there were probably 100 people in attendance. Bob kept walking around reading people's name tags and looking for mine. Whenever I saw him getting close, I would slide away. Finally, I was absorbed in a conversation and lost track of where Bob was. He walked right up to where I was standing. I was caught! Bob talked with me, although it wasn't much of a conversation. I must admit that I was not at all impressed.

Sometime after the party Bob called me and we had a long talk. I decided my first impression was not accurate. We began dating November 1, 1966, and were married in August, 1970. The rest is history.

Secrets for Success:

1. Keep Christ front and center in your life. He can get you through all life's difficulties, and there *will* be difficulties.

2. Grow closer together through the years. Your children will come and years later they will go. But you will still have each other (God willing).

3. Love, honor and respect one another through it all.

Chris & Ann, as told by both

Ann: We first met in seventh grade, where we were placed in the same classes together, except for physical education, then and for the next three years. Chris was a boisterous young boy, one who might be known as the "class clown." I was a bit shy and found his behavior immature and annoying. I was disappointed when he showed up at the same summer church camp I attended. That week I found him obnoxious, especially when he cannon-balled a friend and me in the pool daily!

Chris was very active in sports, while I spent most of my time in choir, band, clubs, church activities and studying. The jocks at school referred to me and my friends as the "bookers!" About half way through ninth grade, Chris began to mature a little and I thought he had become a nice guy. I told one of my close friends that I was starting to like him and would enjoy dating him. Well my friend wasted no time writing Chris a note telling him that I liked him. No texting or Twitter in those days! This was 1966.

Chris: When I received the note from Ann's friend, I was not sure I wanted to be Ann's boyfriend. While I took my studies seriously, I was no "booker." I was very much into football and other sports and fun activities. But there was just something about those dimples that kept my eyes focused on Ann during most of our classes together. I began to be drawn to her. After a few days I told her friend that I would like to become Ann's boyfriend. Due to the rules at my house, I was not permitted to call girls on the phone. Ann was also from a strict home. Casual dating was not encouraged. So the only time we were able to communicate was at school. Our relationship started out very slowly, but we became good friends. We enjoyed extracurricular activities and walking to class together while I carried Ann's books. We discovered we had a lot of similar interests. Our first date was a school-sponsored dance in the cafeteria of Glenwood Junior High School. Ann looked so beautiful that evening. I'm pretty sure that was the day that I actually fell in love with her.

During the summer of 1968 (between our sophomore and junior years), my family took a two week vacation to the western United States. That was very difficult trip for me. By then I was sure I was in love with Ann. I thought that taking me away from her for two weeks (no cell phones!), was just about the worst thing that my family could do to me. Also, I had just learned to drive and was very frustrated that my parents would not let me drive more during the trip.

Ann: We continued to "go steady" until midway through our senior year of high school. In the winter of 1970, I decided that I was sorry that I had maintained an exclusive relationship with one boy throughout my high school years. I broke up with Chris.

Chris: I was devastated and did not understand Ann's feelings or intent. We remained apart for the balance of our senior year and did not attend the senior prom as a couple. We both dated other people. By graduation, Ann had committed to attend Riverside School of Nursing in Toledo, Ohio. I had decided to pursue a teaching career at the University of Toledo, having finally abandoned my dream of becoming an NFL quarterback! Before I would go off to college in the fall of 1970, that summer I worked as a gas station attendant (remember when there was no "self serve"?) One day I looked up and saw Ann and her mother sitting in their car waiting for the attendant (me!) to get to their vehicle to pump their gas and clean their windshield. Ann chatted with me while I cleaned the windshield and suggested we get together before we both left for college. I quickly agreed. What joy came to my heart. After completing my shift, I went home. My mother was sitting down. I picked her up, lawn chair and all, and swung her around and cried out, "I got her back! I got her back! Ann is back!" We have never been "apart" since then. My mom still talks about that.

I proposed to Ann in November, 1971, but both of us (and our parents) wanted to be sure that our education was completed before we married, so we did not plan a wedding at that time. As our relationship grew, we knew we could not wait until I graduated from college. Ann's nursing school was a three year program, so we began to

83

make plans to be wed in the summer of 1973, after Ann's graduation.

We were married in Findlay, Ohio, on June 30, 1973 at 11:30 am. I was sorry that my father had died of a sudden heart attack in June of 1971 and was not able to attend the ceremony. But he saw it all from his vantage point in Heaven. Morning weddings were practically unheard of in our town at that time. My mother did not like the idea at all and threatened to boycott the wedding, since she was normally on the golf course at that time of day. Mother began to learn that she was not going to come between us. We told her that her plan was fine, and that we would see her when we returned from our honeymoon. We say this not to be mean toward her, but because that incident marks one of our keys to maintaining our relationship for over 40 years. There were other episodes of my mother attempting to get more of my attention in circumstances that would have jeopardized my relationship with my bride. Finally, at one critical juncture, I went to my mother and confronted her directly in a loving and caring manner, indicating that if she continued to create these dilemmas for me, she would quickly learn that she would be completely alone, because Ann was now my wife and my first responsibility.

Secrets for Success: There are several reasons why we have been able to stay in love and grow more in love over these past 40 + years. First and foremost is the fact that we enjoy a "tripod relationship." The third leg of our relationship (chair) is Jesus Christ. (Without the third leg, the chair would fall.) We strive to see each other through the eyes of Jesus and to love each other as much as we love ourselves and Jesus.

We have respect for each other. Neither one of us believes that he or she is better than the other. Simple matters like not leaving dirty dishes lying around, putting dirty laundry in the clothes hamper, putting tools back as soon as possible after use, have all been important expectations that have developed into habits in our relationship.

Communication has been a core value for us. Although I do not talk as much as Ann does, we still communicate with each other. In fact, when we were in the trenches raising four children born within six years, at least once each year we planned and executed a "get away weekend." This involved one or both of us planning a trip out of town together without the children. On these trips we refreshed our commitment to each other and we discussed the plans, both current and long-term, for raising our children. Our goal was to identify, and then address, the uniqueness of each child through our parenting.

Now we enjoy walking with each other, usually two to four times a week for a period of 30 to 60 minutes. Not only are we doing something to stay healthy, but we enjoy our time together, sharing our lives with each other. We both state, without hesitation, that our spouse is our best friend.

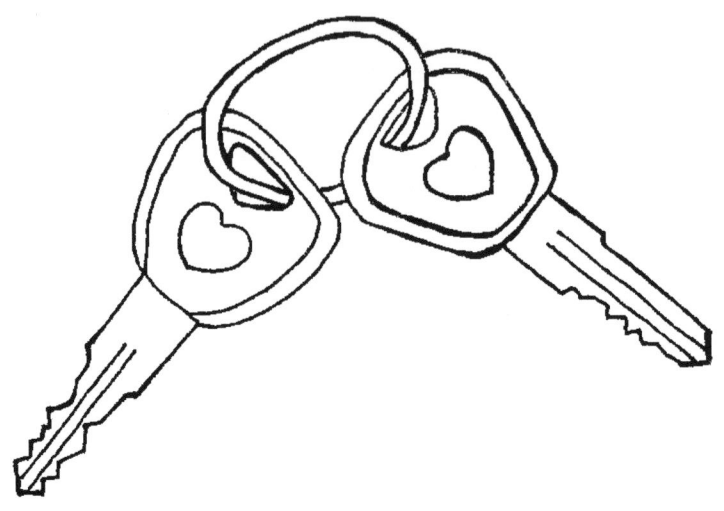

Geoff & Linda, as told by Linda

Geoff and I met in 1968 on a Friday afternoon during Spring Quarter at Baldwin-Wallace College in Berea, Ohio. He had locked his keys in his new car, a green VW Fastback. Geoff has always taken great care of his cars. In this case he didn't want to damage his new toy when he had a spare set of keys at home in Elyria, Ohio. The problem was how to get them. Most of his fraternity brothers were out and about or had lent their cars already. One brother, however, knew that I had just gotten my "new to me" used Mustang on campus so that I could begin my student teaching. The "twosome" came to my dorm to try and convince me to lend them my car so they could drive to Elyria and back, 30 miles each way. It should be noted here that all three of us had dates scheduled with other people for that evening. Not being all that trusting, I refused to let the car go anywhere without me. This trip to Elyria proved to be our first of many adventures together. I even met my future mother-in-law that day.

Geoff proposed to me about 18 months later, early on Christmas morning, 1969, after we attended Christmas Eve Services. We were married seven months later at St. John's Episcopal Church in Cuyahoga Falls, on July 25, 1970.

We have had many ups and downs, as all couples do, and lots of fantastic adventures. I know I made the right choice when I let them talk me into going to Elyria that day.

Secrets for Success: So here we are 43 years later and wondering why that is. We like being together. We are each other's friend. I go to hardware stores with him and he goes to fabric shops with me. We put each other first. We love each other and the daily adventures we have together.

Joseph & Lorrie, as told by Joe

Back when we attended college, the various fraternities and sororities had designated tables in the Student Union where members gathered. Our fraternity, Alpha Sigma Phi, had the table next to the table occupied by Pi Beta Phi, a sorority. This was at the University of Toledo in Ohio.

One of my fraternity brothers, Jeff, and I would take turns doing a "good cop, bad cop" routine when we saw a cute girl. One of us would make a somewhat obnoxious comment, and the other would try to smooth things over. Well, on this particular day in 1969, which I remember very, very well, it was my turn to be the good cop. A Pi Beta Phi named Debbie brought Lorrie to their table. Debbie was older than Lorrie, but she knew her from Whitmer High School, so she was introducing Lorrie to her sorority sisters.

When Jeff and I saw Lorrie, we sprang into action. Jeff made a cat call at her, and I approached her and said "don't pay any attention to my friend." I then introduced myself, said "hi" to Debbie, who I was friends with, and started talking to Lorrie. We talked for awhile, and then I asked her out. She said "yes."

Our first date found us doubling with Jeff. We decided to drive to the airport to watch planes come in. (We really laugh about that now.) It was a bit awkward because Jeff was in the back seat with a student nurse from Toledo Hospital, making out, among other things, just about the entire time. I was trying to have a conversation with Lorrie amid the noise coming from two feet behind us, to say nothing of the steamed up windows that made it difficult to even see the few planes that landed or took off from our small, local airport!

Thankfully, Lorrie didn't judge me by the actions of my friend. When I walked her to the door of her parents' home later that night, I asked Lorrie if she wanted to go out next week. Remarkably, she agreed. Needless to say, we didn't double with Jeff. As I reviewed this story with Lorrie, she reminded me that we eventually dropped off the two disheveled occupants of the car's back seat, and the two of us made our way to Frisch's Big Boy Restaurant on Secor Road. When Lorrie ordered a Big Boy, I thought she was addressing me. (OK, the "Big Boy" part is made up, but all the rest is true.)

Four years later we were married, and this past year was our 40th wedding anniversary. Who knows what would have happened if it had been my turn to be the bad cop!

Secrets for Success: In our case, we'd say the keys were respecting each other, sharing values, agreeing on goals, and listening closely and well to your spouse's concerns on a variety of issues, such as working, intimacy, child rearing, etc. (For example: What's the real concern? Do I understand it? What's the other person's point of view?) Not to be dismissed is the idea of maintaining and appreciating relationships with in-laws. That added such a positive dimension to our lives, and the lives of our children. The importance of same sex friendships should never be overlooked. Good friends were and are incredibly important. Additionally, a shared faith was so meaningful to us. From that so many things sprang.

For us, the most important shared value, besides love for each other and love and support for our children and parents, centered on financial concerns. We were always respectful of each other's individual needs, but those needs never were more important than the goals we agreed upon as a couple: paying for our children's educations, grade school through college; buying our first home; agreeing when it was time to move to a larger home; buying a vacation home; investing; etc. For us, the keys were budgeting, sacrificing when necessary, and delayed gratification. We learned early in our marriage that it was one thing how much money we made for a living, but entirely another thing how we prioritized our spending. (We were often astounded at how much more we had than friends who were making more money than us!) Prior to getting married, we had agreed that our incomes, for the most part, would be pooled. Now, 40 years later, looking back, we can safely say, it worked on a grand scale.

In summary, love, mutual respect, common goals, and a shared belief system worked for us.

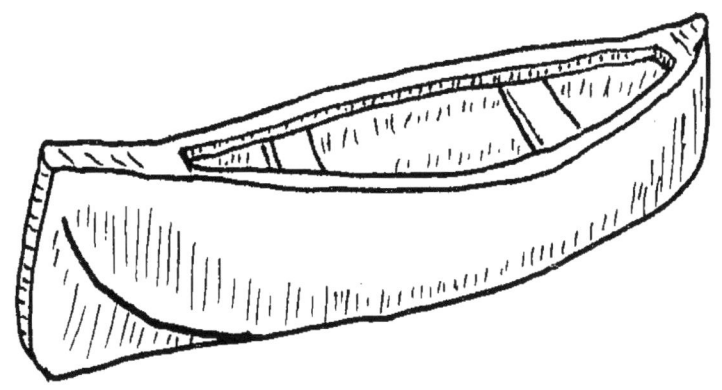

Bruce & Jaclyn, as told by Jaclyn

Our families grew up in the same neighborhood in Sylvania Township, Ohio, known as "Dog Patch." Our families also happened to both vacation in the summer at Vineyard Lake in Michigan. Even though our two families did things together, Bruce and I never really knew each other in the 1960s. We knew OF each other, because our siblings hung out together, but the two of us never really spent any time alone together back then.

I remember Bruce's brother and his wife, because they would always camp at Vineyard Lake right on the beach. They were too cheap to buy a tent! Bruce remembers spending time playing baseball there during the summers.

Although he claims not to remember telling me this now, at one point Bruce confessed that he had dated one of my sisters for a little while, just to get my attention. I really wasn't interested in him at the time.

91

One afternoon in July, 1970, our two families were together looking through pictures of some property in the neighborhood. I noticed Bruce had a girl sitting on his lap. That was it. I knew I didn't like that at all and he was going to have to be my boyfriend. We went out on a date. At the end of the evening, Bruce kept me in the car until I kissed him. We were married five months later, in December of that same year. We have been married for 43 years. We have lived through a house fire, the death of a child, the deaths of our parents, and the death of a grandchild.

Secrets for Success:

First, supporting and being there for each other at all times, in good times and in bad times. We've had a lot of bad times, but we worked through them.

We like being with each other for everything that we do.

Also, we shared everything. Things and money were never "his" or "mine." Everything was "ours." I think not sharing enough is a problem today's couples have.

Steven & Patricia, as told by Steven

I attended Davis Business College in my home town, Toledo, Ohio, majoring in Marketing and Accounting. One fine spring day in 1970 I was walking down the hall and passed a young woman from the Executive Secretarial program working in the college office as part of her student scholarship. I looked at her there sitting at that typewriter, turned to my best friend and said, *"She is the most beautiful girl I have ever seen. I really want to meet her!"* I checked with everyone to find out who she was. Her name was Patricia. She did not hang out much socially with other students, but mostly worked at school and studied. I did find out that she was from a small town, Kalida, in Putnam County, and roomed at Flower Esther Hall. I would hang around and try to talk to her, but she was very shy. Finally, my friend and I came up with a plan. We would kidnap Pat, take her out to the Club 21 bar where we hung out, and then deliver her safely to her home. She, of course, was scared of us, being a smart young woman, but some of the folks in the school administration vouched for us and told her that she would be fine. That was the beginning of a fantastic courtship. We rapidly became inseparable, spending all our free time together.

Finally the day came for me to meet Pat's parents. Pat came from a small farm community that was predominantly Catholic. I was a Jewish boy who was city born and bred. We drove out to her parents' farm, about an hour and a half away. To say I was uncomfortable was an understatement. Pat's parents were just as uncomfortable. Pat had four brother and sisters, the youngest of which were about 9 and 11. They giggled and whispered all through dinner. But by the end, all was good and apparently I became accepted. After that, a normal fun courtship resumed, until I was drafted that same year and inducted into the Army. I left for the service and came home for graduation. Both Pat and I graduated in 1971. In fact, coincidentally, we were chosen as the Outstanding Man of the Year and Outstanding Woman of the Year, and we walked into graduation together leading the class.

Pat was a true support to me during basic training. My permanent assignment was at Fort Knox, Kentucky, about six hours from Toledo if you drove straight through. I tried to get home every possible weekend by using buses, trains, begging rides and even frequently hitchhiking. Many times I would get home with no money and have to beg money from my 90 year old grandma to get back. Fortunately, Grandma and Pat had a special bond, so this worked well!

Pat got a job as a secretary at a major Toledo corporation, the world headquarters of Champion Spark Plug. Eventually I was deployed to Korea for seven months. Letters were exchanged every day, and two very special phone calls even took place.

In September, 1972, I was discharged from active duty to the reserves for four more years. I immediately resumed my education at Findlay College. Eventually the proposal and wedding plans came. The wedding took place in Pat's home town on August 31, 1973—a day that turned out to be 104 degrees in the shade. A college roommate was our vocalist, and the wedding was beautiful. However, on a day described as "the day the city came to Kalida," many occurrences punctuated the event. The air conditioning blew up in the car transporting the bride and groom; all the wedding party cars were ticketed for illegal parking; the top layer of the wedding cake was dropped; and a fraternity brother wrecked his car after the wedding. We think that day used up all of our bad luck, since Pat and I just celebrated forty years of marital bliss. We raised two wonderful daughters and are enjoying our two grandchildren.

Secrets for Success: Accept that you and your spouse are two different people. Accept your differences and don't let them aggravate you. After all, that was your initial attraction! Life is much better together as a team. Support, respect, have fun together, love!

David & Christine, as told by Christine

While attending Ohio's Bowling Green State University in 1970-1972, I was working in the Chemistry Department to help pay for my school expenses. I had made friends with another student majoring in Chemistry who was from the local area. Her name was Sally and her father owned and operated an automotive parts store. Sally had dated the son of one of her father's good friends and customers for some time before the young man joined the Air Force. This young man, David, had attended Defiance College for a short time before enlisting. While David was away in the service for about half of his four-year enlistment, Sally met and became engaged to another science major. So when David came home on leave prior to going to Vietnam in 1970, Sally couldn't go out with him and arranged for me to go out with him as a favor to her. Sally chaperoned us on the blind date to help break the ice. During the rest of David's leave, we saw each other every evening after my classes. On his final evening, David handed me a brown paper bag with a small pre-engagement ring in it. The next day he left for a year in Vietnam.

I wrote every day to the address David had given me, but was shocked when the first two weeks of mail came back marked "addressee unknown." It seemed David had been reassigned upon his arrival at Tan Son Nhut Air Base, and his supervisors had forgotten to inform the base post office. Once the snafu was straightened out, David received a backlog of letters which he was finally able to answer. In the first letter, he mentioned that he had forgotten in his nervousness to ask the big question when giving me that first ring. No problem. I was so shocked, I hadn't said anything either.

David's friends in Vietnam kept telling him the courtship had been too quick and that the relationship would never last. They predicted that soon he would get a "Dear John'" letter dumping him. However they were wrong. When you have to put your thoughts and dreams down on paper, you learn a great deal, not only about yourself, but about your correspondent. The letters continued to fly, covering almost every aspect of day-to-day life for both of us, and a deep bond was formed. Not too many people start life together knowing as much about each other.

When David came home on leave after his year in Vietnam, he presented me with an engagement ring. My mother didn't like the idea of my dating a serviceman, let alone planning marriage to one. Too many of her friends hadn't come home from WWII or the Korean War. She felt that as long as David was in the service, we shouldn't even consider engagement. Besides she had other plans for my future. She expressed this opinion and her ideas in many negative ways at every given opportunity. Because of this negativity, I decided to fly down to see David at his current base during my senior year spring break in 1972, at which time we were married. We had gotten the idea from David's parents, who weren't at all opposed to the match. You see it was sort of a family tradition in David's family. Both his father and uncle had served in the Air Force (Army Air Corps at the time) and eloped during WWII.

We are still together over 40 years later. We raised a son who also joined the Air Force and eloped when he met the right young lady. Our wish for him is that he has as many happy years as we have already had and continue to enjoy.

Secrets for Success:

1. Say I love you (or demonstrate it) when it isn't connected to anything else, like a request or after an action. It has to be for absolutely no reason other than you love each other.
2. Use "please" and "thank you," even for the little things.
3. Laugh! Laugh! Laugh! It's easier than getting mad and your blood pressure will be lower, making for a longer life together.
4. Never contradict your spouse in public. Wait until you get home and then do it in a polite and tactful manner: "Honey, I think if you will look into that more you may find that . . ."
5. Support each others' interests even if it bores you to tears.
6. Accept that God created relatives about which your spouse had no choice and may not even like. There are those who will be welcome; some who will be tolerated; and some you can ignore.
7. Repeat #1 often.

$$f(x) = a^*x^2 + d$$

Dan and Sue, as told by Dan

Some people might call it "luck" or "good fortune." Others might call it "fate." Was it "kismet?" Or maybe it was just the "Will of God." Whatever it was, just one little event in my daily life changed everything, forever. At the time, of course, I had no idea as to the degree of significance of this event, but it caused my life to take a major change in direction.

When I was seventeen, and looking for a job, I decided to apply at a Churchill's grocery store. It was located between my home in Toledo, Ohio, and my high school, St. Francis de Sales. Included among the other basic employment application forms was a questionnaire asking about my likes and interests. I filled it out and left. After a period of time when I hadn't heard anything concerning my application, my mom contacted a friend of hers who worked at a Foodtown grocery store and told her that I was looking for a job. The friend directed me to their store located at Alexis and Clover Lane, where I was hired as a carryout.

While working at Foodtown, another carryout, Ray, told me that he knew a girl, Sue, who would like to meet me. Sue would often bring her mom to the store to shop and she had seen me working there. In time we were introduced. That was 1971. I was on the St. Francis football team and our first game was against Whitmer High School, where she went to school. We made a bet on the outcome of the game, with the "loser" having to make dinner for the winner. I won. (That is a bet we have continued for many years.) Sue and I dated for a few months, broke up for awhile, and then got back together the following Easter. We have been together ever since, now married over 41 years!

What was that "little event" that changed my life forever? It was NOT getting hired at Churchill's. (What's that song about unanswered prayers?) I'm certain that I never would have crossed paths with Sue if I had been hired at Churchill's, in a completely different area of town from Foodtown. We were also from basically different life styles. She was studying cosmetology in public school, while I was taking college prep classes and had plans on attending college for engineering. Religion had a very strong influence in my life, and I attended Catholic grade school and high school. Attending church weekly was a "given." In Sue's life, religion did not have that same priority. We both did share a strong family base, but each with its own unique style.

100

Why wasn't I hired at Churchill's? I found out the reason later from my sister's friend, who worked there. The questionnaire asked about "hobbies." I answered that question by saying that I enjoyed solving math problems. At that time I was taking an advanced calculus class my senior year and had always enjoyed the challenge of solving mathematical problems. When my employment application was reviewed, someone interpreted my answer as "he has a problem with math." That "little" misunderstanding, through fate, or in this case "good fortune," changed the direction of my life forever. I have never regretted it!

Secrets for Success: While marriage has to be a mutual give and take, fifty-fifty, you have to be willing to give 100 percent, and give it 100 percent of the time. Don't keep "score" - always want to give more.

Kevin & Lynn, as told by Lynn

Kevin and I met on a blind date. We had both graduated from different colleges and were working in our hometown of Toledo, Ohio. A mutual friend of ours,

Bruce, thought we would be a good match. I had literally grown up with Bruce. Our parents went to high school together and started raising families at the same time.

Bruce and Kevin were Theta Chi fraternity brothers at the University of Toledo. Their friendship continued beyond graduation and is still maintained today, over forty years later. At the time Bruce suggested that Kevin and I meet, I had recently broken up with my "college boyfriend" and was slowly entering the dating pool. Bruce made the arrangements for the date in the fall of 1974. Being a fashion maven, I was wearing my hair in a huge Afro at the time, which easily added 3" to my height of 5' 9". After I agreed to the date, Bruce informed me that Kevin was also 5' 9". Thus began my rush to buy a pair of flats for our first date.

Kevin and I went to dinner and later to a local hotel lounge for drinks and dancing, which was the "thing to do" back in the day. I had a pleasant time, but I was taken aback by how quiet Kevin was. I figured he didn't enjoy himself and I'd never hear from him again. Imagine my surprise when I got a call for another date! We continued to see each other on a regular basis, but I "was running out of gas," so to speak. I would come home after a date totally exhausted. It took me several weeks to figure out what the problem was. Kevin was beyond "quiet." He barely spoke. Therefore I basically had to carry on the conversation for two people! I had reached the point where I decided I really couldn't do this anymore. My decision must have been telepathic, because after I made up my mind to stop seeing him, Kevin started to talk!

Kevin proposed by handing me a ring box. My heart racing, I opened it. Inside was a very unusual gold ring with a diamond. Kevin didn't say a word. Not wanting to be made a fool by jumping to the wrong conclusion (we had never talked about marriage or looked at rings), I asked him what this was. His response was "What do you think it is?" As I recall, he finally identified the ring as an engagement ring. And thus began the union of Mr. Romance and me. Thirty seven years later Kevin is still pretty quiet and every bit as confusing to me as he was back then!

Secrets for Success: I think the single most important thing in making a relationship work is communication. Most of us are not mind readers. You may believe you know what your spouse is thinking, feeling, or believing, but why not ask and find out? Too many arguments are started by misunderstandings related to the lack of communication or miscommunication.

There is a popular saying that goes something like this: *"I know that you believe you understand what you think I said, but I'm not sure you realize that what you heard is not what I meant."* This comment has been attributed to two different Robert McCloskeys, Jerry Lewis, Alan Greenspan, and even Richard Nixon, in many contexts. *But it is never truer than in a marriage!*

Also, don't be afraid to:

- Laugh at yourself and also try to find humor in the bumps in the road.
- Cry, whether it's from sorrow or happiness.
- Speak your mind. If you never disagree, someone is giving in all the time.

Greg & Kathy, as told by Kathy

Greg and I lived in the same small town in Ohio and went to the same high school. Greg's dad and my mom worked at the same place, and our grandparents were also good friends. Yet we never formally met. It took my friend, Linda, who later became my sister-in-law, to get us together.

Greg's life always revolved around sports. So when he wasn't coaching, he spent most of his free time going to sporting events or just being a spectator on his parents' couch. As Linda visited Greg's brother one day, Greg surprised her by asking, "Do you have any nice friends?" Linda sensed that Greg wanted to be "fixed up" with

105

someone. Linda immediately thought of me, someone she hadn't seen for some time.

In November, 1975, Linda called me to inquire about my dating status and she asked if I would mind having Greg call me. We arranged to go out. Greg planned QUITE a first date. It was a marathon. He took me to a college football game. Then we went out to dinner. Then we went to "Holiday On Ice," which was a figure skating show at the hockey arena in Toledo involving music, lights, costumes, and stories. We enjoyed each other's company and found that we had many things in common, especially our teaching professions. We soon started dating steadily and then, seven months later, Greg surprised me by asking, "Will you marry me?" We married in July, 1977.

During our 36 years of marriage, we raised one successful son and two spoiled dogs. We both retired after completing a total of 67 years teaching in the public schools. Now we are focusing more on enriching our lives with more family time, travel, volunteering, and simply trying to make the world a better place! "Life is good!"

Secrets for Success: Staying together takes patience and understanding and the realization that you have to work hard at all things in order to be successful. Our world is such a "throw away" society, some people now find it convenient to just "delete" things from their lives, much like they do on a computer. When conflict arises in a relationship, we believe it is necessary to talk things over, see each other's point of view, admit when you're wrong, and not hold a grudge...and NEVER go to bed angry! Our faith, prayer, and laughter have truly helped us through some difficult times. It also helps to ask yourself: "Is this going to be important to us tomorrow? Next week? Next month? Next year?" Try to see an amusing, funny side to difficult situations because it really does help to LAUGH together! Appreciate the precious time you have together...it really goes fast!

Brian & Debbie, as told by Debbie

We actually first met on the telephone. In 1978 I was working days full time as a legal secretary and going to college at nights. My best friend was getting married in September, and she asked me to be her maid of honor. I wanted to have the "bachelorette party" for the bride on the same night as the bachelor party for the groom. In August I asked the bride to give me the name and phone number of the best man, who I had never met. I called this "Brian" person, introduced myself, and asked what night he was going to throw the bachelor party. He hadn't decided yet! I was not happy about that. Chop, chop! Time is short! But we chit-chatted some more and I was really drawn to his voice and sense of humor.

A few days later, Brian called me back. I can't remember exactly how this worked out, but either he could not get a party date set or we both found excuses to keep calling each other for what became some pretty long conversations. Finally Brian asked me to lunch—a nice safe first date. After that, there were more long phone calls and then the wedding rehearsal, the rehearsal dinner, and the wedding. We never told the bride and groom we had met. While the happy couple was away on their honeymoon, we rendezvoused to booby trap their apartment (a custom back then), and had a few dates. By the time our friends returned home, our fate was sealed, and they didn't even know we were dating! Later our two best friends explained that they had never fixed us up because they thought we were polar opposites. I guess they did not know that opposites attract.

One evening after class the following May, Brian was at my apartment. We were watching TV. It started raining, so he got up and closed my living room window. Later we turned off the TV, turned out the lights in the living room and headed to the back door area of my apartment to kiss goodnight. I heard the wind chimes blow in that same living room window. I said "Didn't you shut that window?" Brian said that he thought he did, but "let's go check." He went ahead of me and crossed the living room to the window, but I lingered in the doorway to flip on the overhead light for him. When I did, I saw that hunkered down on a love seat within arm's reach of me, with Brian maybe 16 feet away from both of us, was an intruder!! Now mine was a second story apartment, it was pouring rain, and this man's clothes were completely dry. When I later regained my senses, I realized that to have dry clothes, he had to have been sitting out on an adjoining roof section under an overhang for some time, watching us watch TV! After we turned out the lights and left the room, he waited a few minutes, opened the window (that had no lock), and climbed in.

Needless to say, Brian saved me that night. Within two weeks an intruder broke into another apartment in my building at night and committed violent criminal acts on the female tenant. The police believed it was the same man and that he had mistaken my apartment for hers.

Well after <u>that</u> I could not sleep in my apartment! The least little noise made my heart race and my adrenaline flow. I started shopping for a new apartment, but quickly realized the better neighborhoods cost double or triple my rent. My plight apparently inspired Brian to propose marriage, on the Fourth of July, 1979. I was so shocked that I asked him if I could think about it!

October 6, 1979, was the only open Saturday all fall in Brian's football officiating schedule, so that had to be our wedding date under our time constraints to get me out of that apartment quickly. We found an apartment we both liked, and I moved in first. We only had three months to make all the wedding arrangements. Brian is Catholic and I am Protestant. We learned my conversion to his faith would have taken over a year and, without it, we could not get married in his Catholic church in Toledo. My Protestant church was in a town two and a half hours from his family and our friends. So we were married by my minister in my parents' home, halfway in between in Milan, Ohio, with only immediate family present—and of course the bride and groom in whose wedding we met, who now were <u>our</u> best man and matron of honor.

After the ceremony we had a luncheon at a nearby resort, and then had everyone come back to my parents' house for a dessert reception. Small and simple. Affordable. My only "regrets," if you can even call them that, were that we didn't have a wedding cake and we didn't get to dance at our wedding. Oh well. No big deal, right?

Later, Brian and I drove to our wedding night hotel in Sandusky. We found the lights out and the door locked with a sign, "Closed for Plumbing Repairs. Try our other location." What? Imagine the look on our faces! Much later we found the "other location" (in the dark, in a strange town, without cell phones or GPS) and checked in to our room. I pretty much collapsed in exhaustion. It was then that I felt sort of sick and realized that I had not eaten since noon. My sweet groom went back out to get me a sandwich at Arby's!

For our 25th wedding anniversary in 2004, we decided to renew our vows, this time in the Catholic faith. It wound up being really, REALLY Catholic, as we were remarried in Italy by a priest who spoke only Latin and Italian. We learned that the financial patrons of that particular church were the Vespucci family. Amerigo Vespucci, the explorer and navigator, was a local, historical celebrity, believed to have been a part of the discovery of "the Americas." The little old ladies who came to say rosaries and stayed for our wedding were all aflutter over the fact that we *Americans* had come to *their church* to be wed.

The ceremony was on a Friday, which was the last day of our week of cooking school in Tuscany. That night the Italian chefs, Roberto and Elvio, and the tour guides and interpreters, Karen and Linda, gave us a surprise wedding dinner in a private room of the restaurant. Stephan, a waiter, made us a mix cassette tape. So 25 years later we finally had our wedding cake and wedding dance! We asked these five new friends and a few others to join us. After some champagne and a lot of laughter, I asked Elvio how he met his wife, my favorite conversation. He explained in Italian, while Karen and Linda interpreted. By the time he was done, everyone in the room was in tears. Love, friendship, sentiment, good food and great wine have universal appeal. This year will be our 35th anniversary. Brian is still my hero.

111

Secrets for Success:

1. Marry your best friend. If you'd rather spend your time with him than anyone else on the planet, girlfriends and other family included, he's your keeper. Friends, siblings, and co-workers will come and go or move away, and children are meant to grow up and have their own lives.

2. Before you choose a spouse, watch how he or she treats both sets of your parents and siblings, illness, adversity, and all children, elderly, or animals. You can tell a lot about a person that way.

3. Don't cross the line. Once said in anger, some things can never be *forgotten*, even if they are forgiven.

4. Don't keep score. So you're annoyed he never puts the newspaper away, tackles the pile of mail, or prepares the income tax info? Well, he shovels snow when it is 10 degrees out and mows lawn when it is 90 and humid! Wanna trade jobs with him? Just each do all that you can, according to your abilities. Be a team.

5. Don't do anything that would cause either of you to lose respect for the other. How can you be happily married to someone you don't respect?

6. Spend more time preparing for the *marriage* than planning for the *wedding*.

7. Lastly, here's what my mother told me: "Don't you *dare* marry someone and expect to change them!"

Fred & Lynda, as told by Lynda

In 1978 I was working at Higbee's Department Store in the shopping mall in Elyria, Ohio, as the manager of china, crystal, gifts and home accessories. Fred got a new job there as manager of budget men's clothing. The first time I saw Fred he was wearing a mauve suit and one inch heels (this was the '70's). At some point I mentioned Fred's full name to my mother, who replied that she knew of him. She explained that my father's sister's husband was a "golf and drinking buddy" of Fred's father. Since my parents knew Fred's parents, somehow we introduced ourselves to each other at work. This was retail, and sometimes we both had to work the late shift. We might bump into each other at dinner in Higbee's Attic Restaurant or in group dinners at the employee cafeteria. Then the shopping mall sponsored an "Olympic" event, and each store entered a team of employees to compete. The challenge of one event was to see how many people you could get on a small raised platform at one time (sort of like "how many people can you get in a phone booth?"). Fred managed to get his arms around me in that melee so we could squeeze into a tighter group. Later Fred offered me a ride home, and after that we started dating. This was 1979. Dates included movies, dinners, polka dancing and theater.

Fred lived in an apartment, and I noticed that he kept his Christmas tree up all year long. I decided he seriously needed my help. We bought a condo together for him to move in. I then sold the entire contents of his apartment at a garage sale. Fred quit his job at Higbee's and took a job selling Yellow Pages advertising. He traveled all week and came home on the weekends. We were getting used to each other and trying to meld our two independent lives. I used to tell Fred, "How can I grieve if you won't leave? How can I miss you if you won't go away?" During this time period of Fred's traveling, we were also rehabbing the condo. I would stay at my parents' house on weekdays and at the condo on weekends. My parents didn't approve of this at all, but Fred treated me well and was especially nice to my father. My parents finally gave in and accepted the relationship on a cautionary basis.

In 1985 we bought our current home. The plan was for both of us to live there together and rent out the condo, but somehow I never quite moved in. Then in 1992 my parents sold their home, so I finally moved in with Fred. Around December of 2000, after 22 years of dating, and several years of being engaged, when we were both age 58, we decided to elope, in order to avoid a big party. We were already scheduled for a vacation on the Mississippi Queen, consisting of a paddlewheel cruise of the Mississippi River from New Orleans to Natchez and back. We thought the ship's captain could marry us on our trip. Well, that's true of a ship at sea, but not one on a river! Through phone calls beforehand, the cruise line connected us with a "good old boy" Justice of the Peace in Natchez. While the ship was docked there, he got the three day blood test waived and expedited the courthouse paperwork. Since we missed the cruise ship side-trip itinerary for the day, namely the bus tour of Natchez, he even drove us around and showed us the town, including introducing us to a Senator passing by in the courthouse. Finally the three of us boarded the ship for the ceremony.

We had planned to say "I do" in the ship's Paddlewheel Lounge, with just us and one other couple as our witnesses, our friends, Dan and Carolyn. Somehow word leaked out of an on-board wedding, and it seemed like the whole passenger list showed up! The law was that as long as the ship was docked, no alcohol could be sold. You couldn't *sell* it, but you could *serve* it. Fred had told the bartender to run a tab and keep the champagne coming, thinking there were only going to be the five of us partaking. When 150 or more showed up, he looked a little pale. But we never saw a check for that champagne! Bill, the president of our bank that was our travel club's sponsor, picked up the tab. The date was February 21, 2001, which was Fat Tuesday or Mardi Gras Day. The cruise line surprised us with a cake. It was a traditional "King's Cake," which has a toy baby inside. The frosting had trim in Mardi Gras colors: green for faith, purple for justice, and gold for power. The next day, for our honeymoon, we went on the day's tour of a swamp!

Although married now for 13 years, we've been together for 35 years. We've seen each other through parental illnesses and loss, career trials and tribulations, and surgeries; remodeled several properties; and traveled extensively around the world, including China, Russia, the Galapagos Islands, the Caribbean, the Canadian Rockies, Alaska, and throughout Europe.

Secrets for Success:

Lynda says: Share the joy in doing things together, but also do your own thing. Pursue your own interests. Kick him out of the house every now and then to go play golf and tell him not to come home for at least five hours. It helps to have a sense of humor and to develop selective hearing. It also is a big help to not care about the small stuff. If he wants to wear that old stretched out of shape sweatshirt out in public, let him, as long as he is not going with you.

Fred says: We are peas out of the same pod. The only problem is that she likes peas and I don't. We both agree that time spent together is important, but equally, as well, those times apart are necessary to pursue your own interests. We each have our favorite pastimes, but look forward to doing things together. You could say that we are the best of friends.

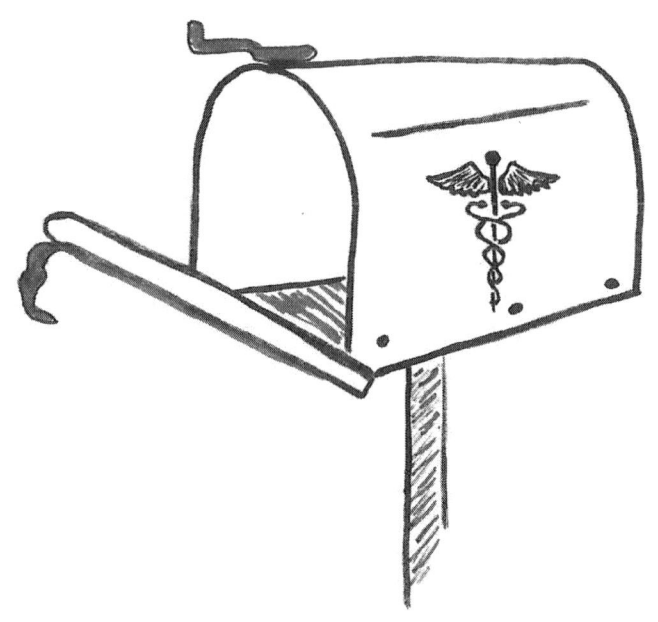

Duane & Maria, as told by Duane

We actually met at a medical conference in 1979. Maria was the director of the Guadalupe Health Clinic in the old south end of Toledo, Ohio, and she had organized the conference. At the time I was a medical student at the University of Pennsylvania and had an interest in the topic, so I registered to attend this weekend conference, which was held in Toledo. After the conference I was more enthralled with the conference organizer than with the conference itself. Wanting more information, I sent a letter to Maria, which was also an excuse to start communicating with her!

The two of us began having regular telephone conversations. We arranged to get together over the New Year holiday to get to know one another better. I remember that upon my arrival, Maria asked me to wait at a Catholic outdoor shrine, in the middle of rural Ohio, in the middle of winter, while she went to ask her father's permission to bring me to their home. I waited, prayed, and shivered until she returned. This moment began the process of learning how different our two upbringings were. Soon, we started courting. Later that year she had the opportunity to come to California, where I was raised, although I didn't take her to a Methodist shrine, but only to the church where I was raised.

Maria was divorced and the mother of two children. I knew right away that she was a good woman, just by the way she interacted with her children. We dated one and a half years, even though we lived 500 miles apart. Once we decided to get married, Maria informed me that she had already had one wedding: if I wanted a wedding, I would have to plan it! Plan it I did, and our wedding actually involved seven pastors, either directly or indirectly. Maria quit her job to move with me as a medical resident, which required us to move to Arizona, then to Texas, and finally to Ohio. This summer will be our 33rd wedding anniversary.

***Secrets for Success*:** In the beginning, it was faith and prayer that ultimately helped us to get through some difficult times. Humor helped, as well as some counseling on conflicts over our cultural and economic differences and the different ways we were raised by our parents. Eventually we developed an appreciation for and became involved in each other's worlds. Our success also required both of us to sacrifice some activities that we enjoyed—for Maria, dancing, and for me, primitive camping. We learned the art of compromise, sacrifice and recognizing and remembering what is really important.

You asked for advice for young couples. I would say that in the quest for a life partner, one should evaluate what the person's relationship is with their parents, especially a boy with his mother and a girl with her father. I would also caution couples to not have an early sexual relationship. When we allow a relationship to have early sexual roots, it allows sex to become the focus of the relationship. Physical intimacy becomes a replacement for love, instead of intimacy becoming the result of love.

Ken & Diane, as told by Diane

After I graduated from college in 1979, I went back home to live. I didn't have a job at the time. My mother asked me if I would go stay with my grandmother because she broke her arm and needed help. I said "sure" and I moved in over there. After she was healed, grandma didn't want me to leave. We were having fun and she had company every day, so I stayed with her.

The following April, 1980, my very good friend, Sue, told me I had to get out of the house for an evening. She suggested we go "bar hopping." I had never done that before. The first place we stopped was Biddie Mulligan's Pub on Hill and Reynolds in Toledo. We were there for a short time when she started a conversation with three guys. I was instantly attracted to one of them, "Ken." He was there with his brother-in-law, Chris, and Chris' brother, Paul. I thought Ken was the cutest guy I had ever seen. A little while later, we all left in separate cars and went to another place. We sat and talked for quite a while. Ken asked me for my phone number. I gave it to him, wishing and hoping he would call.

Ken never called. I was so crushed. Three months went by. Then I asked Sue if we could go back to Biddie Mulligan's Pub to see if I could bump into Ken again. I really wanted to try to find him. All I knew was his first name. Lo and behold, when we entered the second time, Ken was there, again with Chris and Paul. I was so excited, I could hardly breathe. We talked for quite some time. Ken again asked me for my phone number. This time I played hard to get. I wouldn't give it to him. He told me his mother washed his pants with my phone number inside the pocket. After going back and forth about this several times, Ken asked me "What do I have to do to get your number?" It was then I felt he really meant what he said and that he would call me.

Well, he did. Then two months after Ken's first call, we attended the wedding of my college roommate. After her ceremony was over, Ken said to me, "When I get married, I want you to be standing at the altar next to me."

We were engaged seven months later and married nine months after that. This year, we celebrate our 32nd wedding anniversary. We have three handsome boys ages 26, 25, and 16. Our boys have been told the importance of calling someone when you say you will!

Secrets for Success: Call me old-fashioned, but I gave my heart to one and only one man, Ken. I can't imagine loving anyone else. It is hard for me to understand people who are able to love multiple persons over time. Both Ken and I stood before God and promised "until death do us part." We NEVER took that for granted. Sure, we have had difficult times, and there were times when I wanted to kick him to the curb. But that feeling never lasted long. (And making up is heavenly!) Vows before God are sacred and neither one of us ever took them lightly. That's what I recommend for newlyweds for the success of their marriage. So put more thought into the nature of the commitment BEFORE you decide who to marry.

Kevin & Kathleen, as told by Kevin

In the fall of 1981, my sister and I were starting our freshman and junior years, respectively, at John Carroll University in University Heights, a suburb of Cleveland, Ohio. I attended some freshman event in my sister's dorm to see how she was getting along. She introduced me to another freshman, Kathleen, who I thought was pretty cute. I made a mental note to stop back and talk to her again, but I never followed through, at least, not intentionally.

A few weeks later I was involved in a fundraiser for my collegiate swim team. Our job was to get "per lap" pledges for a Swimathon, to raise money for my team to go to Florida and train over Christmas break. My roommate, John, suggested that as upper classmen, we might have better luck getting pledges down at the freshman dorm. So we went floor to floor, knocking on doors, asking for sponsors. To my surprise, one of the doors was opened by Kathleen! I tried to make it sound like swimming 5,000 yards was an arduous task, in order to get her pledge. It turns out, though, that she was a swimmer herself and she did not fall for the pitch! She offered me a penny a lap and we bantered back and forth for a while. Somehow I managed to leave my letter jacket in her room. Later that day she tracked me down to return it, and we talked and flirted some more. I learned that at the time, Kathleen was dating her roommate Carla's friend, Todd. (Incidentally, Carla and Todd later got married themselves.)

Kathleen eventually stopped dating Todd and she came to one of my swim meets. We soon started dating. This was toward the end of the fall semester, and then we were together all of spring semester. I went home to Perrysburg, Ohio, to work for the summer, and Kathleen headed home to Port Huron, Michigan. Although we did not have an understanding between us at the time, Kathleen told her parents she had met the man she was going to marry. Her parents' reaction was to tell Kathleen that she was not going back to John Carroll in the fall! Obviously, this was before cell phones, so our long distance telephone bills that summer, and there-after, were enormous. We arranged to call each other at 11:01 p.m., after the long distance rates went down for the night. During some conversation that summer, we decided that I should come up and visit Kathleen and

124

meet her parents. I was saving my pennies, so I didn't want to spend money on a hotel room. But Kathleen's parents would not let me sleep under their roof. I had to take a tent along and sleep alone at a nearby campground!

Kathleen transferred to the University of Michigan in Ann Arbor that fall, and she went there for her next three years through her graduation. I went back to John Carroll for my senior year, and then attended Bowling Green State University in Ohio for my Master's Degree, living at home with my parents in Perrysburg to save money. Kathleen and I only saw each other at holidays and the occasional long weekend over the next three years. Over this entire time period, we never spent more than just a few consecutive days with each other, but we were in love and determined to make this long distance romance work.

In November, 1983, Kathleen was in her junior year of college. I went up to Ann Arbor to visit her for the Ohio State vs. University of Michigan football game. We rooted for opposite teams, so we made a bet that the loser had to take the winner out for dinner. Michigan won, so it was supposed to be my treat. We headed for the Red Lobster in Ann Arbor. I proposed to Kathleen in the car in the parking lot before dinner. She accepted immediately and we went in for a dinner celebration. Much to my chagrin, I discovered that I didn't have enough cash on me for the whole celebration. Kathleen had to chip in on the check, and she complains to this day that I did not pay the full tab. I point out that I gave her an engagement ring that night!

We were married on May 25, 1985, three weeks after Kathleen graduated from Michigan. Our two week honeymoon to Disney and Daytona Beach was the first time we had ever spent more than a few days together. Our choice of each other in her first year at John Carroll and our mutual patience and work with a long distance relationship proved to be the right decisions for us. After 28 years of marriage, three children, and our first grandchild, Kathleen is still my sweetheart, and we wouldn't have our story begin any other way.

Secrets for Success:

1. Communication is key, no matter how hard it is sometimes.

2. You have to set aside your ego and try not to always be "right."

3. Say "I love you" each day.

4. Try, try not to go to bed mad. Work it out as soon as you can.

5. Be honest and genuine with people in general, but especially with your partner in life.

John & Victoria, as told by John

In the summer of 1985, my older sister, Debby, wanted to take a martial arts class. She wanted me to sign up with her. When we joined the class, Victoria and Joe were among the several students we met. The shortest story is that I wound up marrying Victoria and my sister wound up marrying Joe. (So if you want to get married, take a martial arts class!)

This class was held every Wednesday night, and it became a custom for many of the students to go out together afterward to a place called "The Ottawa Tavern," or "The O.T.," for short. This tavern was a neighborhood bar and popular University of Toledo student hang-out. It

127

was pretty casual, so we could practice our techniques in the open areas and laugh and have a great time. The four of us, in particular, among the group started to bond as good friends.

As the months rolled by, it came time for my sister and me to take our test for our first belt. We all went to The O.T. afterward to celebrate. Victoria and I left in our separate cars to head for our respective homes around 11:00 p.m. or shortly thereafter. For a while we were both driving in the same direction. Then we stopped at the traffic light, with our cars side by side, where we would each have to turn in opposite directions. As we were sitting at the red light, Victoria rolled down her window and motioned for me to roll mine down. She asked, "Don't you owe me a cup of coffee?" So we went to Frisch's Big Boy restaurant on Alexis Road and had coffee and talked until 3 a.m.!

That was probably the beginning of our more personal relationship, although we continued to go out in groups and hang out with our friends and classmates. At some point we started going out on Fridays and Saturdays, usually in downtown Toledo, since I worked at a bank there, and back then downtown was a lively place to go. We would eat at Ricardo's, Georgio's, The Real Seafood, etc., and some of these places had dance floors as well. I remember one time Victoria had me over to her house for dinner, and we went outside and walked and talked in the pouring rain afterward.

As long as we were just friends in the larger group, my Mom liked Victoria just fine. But when she learned we were actually dating, her attitude changed. My mom was a strict Catholic, I was the youngest of six children (her "baby"), and Victoria was a divorced mother of three children. I knew this was going to be ticklish with my Mom, from a prior incident in my family in which one of my brothers broke an expectation of strict Catholics. In reaction, my mother locked herself in her bedroom under a cone of silence for a week. At this point in my relationship with Victoria, I had moved out of my parents' home and was sharing an apartment with Joe. I asked him to leave for the night and invited my mother over to cook dinner for her. I explained my feelings for Victoria and told my Mom, "If you make me choose, you are not going to like the answer." From that time on, she was fine with Victoria.

In 1988 we made plans to attend the wedding of Victoria's best friend, Kyle, who was to be married on a yacht in the San Francisco Bay. I realized the location was only about an hour from Pebble Beach Golf Links. I decided I wanted us to play a round there and propose to Victoria on the 18th hole. I reserved a tee time months in advance. That day the bride's mother, Betty, and friend, Sandy, were to complete our foursome and be my co-conspirators for the surprise. I gave the engagement ring to Betty to carry and charged Sandy with videotaping the proposal with a huge camera I rented for the occasion "to document the round of golf."

The Pebble Beach procedure is that you have to call and confirm the reservations 24 hours in advance, or lose them. The day before our reservation, we were in Napa Valley with the wedding party. Time slipped away in all the commotion. When I looked at my watch, I realized it was an hour past the confirmation deadline. I ran to a pay phone to make the call—no cell phones back then. They told me we lost our tee time! No amount of begging and groveling, nor sharing of my Big Plan, could make them budge. Apparently they had heard every excuse in the book before. Eventually they gave us a tee time for a day later in the week, *after* Kyle's wedding. That meant changing a lot of plans in a domino effect.

Our golf day finally arrived and the weather was wonderful. Victoria and I both made par on 18, so we were in a great mood. After the scheduling snafu, things now looked like they were lining up perfectly. I had been filming our round of golf with the video camera, so I handed it to Sandy, according to plan, so she could film the proposal. I asked Victoria the big question, presented the ring to her, and she said "yes." Unfortunately, Sandy was not so compliant! For some reason, she decided to set the video camera down on the golf cart so she could take still photos of the proposal. After the proposal, we all got in our carts and were laughing and celebrating on the ride back to the clubhouse. We did not realize the video camera was still rolling the whole time.

Sometime later we all sat down to enjoy the memorialization of our special moment. We discovered that every still photo Sandy took had our heads lopped off! And there was not one scene of the proposal on the video tape. But by leaving the camera "on" and placing it on the golf cart rack facing the rear, Sandy did manage to capture a nice, long, cartoon-like video of the two golf bag zippers flapping in the breeze during the ride back, as if they were two mouths talking to each other! We all laughed until we cried, including Sandy. Kyle laughed so hard she wet her pants.

Two years later Victoria and I were married. We still have that video tape, 26 years later. Our Pebble Beach score cards from that day are on a plaque hanging on our bedroom wall. My Mom and Victoria grew to love each other. Debby and Joe married each other as well.

Secrets for Success: We are both very good at compromising. We believe in open communication and being open-minded. We are supportive of each other in decisions we each make. As you can tell, we value a sense of humor and laughter. We share common interests, especially golf. We are always there for each other in all problems. We support each other, even when we disagree. When one of us admits we were wrong, the other one doesn't rub it in. We think all these things have contributed to our happiness together.

Tim & Diane, as told by both

Diane's father suspected there was something between us even before we realized there was. Every year he heard our laughter float down the company hallway as we filmed and edited an annual Christmas video together. We were "just friends" and co-workers for six years. Then we started dating one August, became engaged in September, and married in November, just ten weeks later. When Diane called her best friend to tell her that she was going to be married, her friend responded "are you even *dating* anyone??" That was over 21 years ago.

To start at the beginning, Diane's father was President of Davis College in Toledo. He hired Tim in 1987 to teach commercial art. Diane was assigned to conduct Tim's new employee orientation. Tim noted that Diane was attractive, but mentally filed her under "the boss's daughter—hands off." Diane gradually formed the opinion that Tim was intelligent and very cool. But at the college Spring Fling dance, she learned Tim had a girlfriend. So she mentally filed him under "in a relationship—hands off."

So we became friends at work, but did not really socialize together outside of work. We had many opportunities at work to observe each other's personality and character, and to interact. Diane took a seminar Tim taught on desktop publishing. She loved how witty and confident he was. We saw each other at school functions like the fall hayride. Tim always enjoyed seeing Diane smile and experiencing her joyful and enthusiastic nature. He thought Diane loved to have fun, but she always wanted to make sure everyone around her was having fun, too. In 1989 we had a few opportunities to work together creating marketing materials for the Business Training Division that Diane directed. As Diane told Tim of her aspirations for the Division, Tim thought she was intelligent, passionate, and creative. During this time our professional relationship grew stronger and our friend- ship grew closer. We discovered that we had similar interests, including sports and music, and we both valued the importance of family.

We looked back a little later and realized that sparks probably started flying between us as we worked on the 1992 Christmas video. But it still wasn't until August, 1993, that we started dating. After work one night we met at Nick & Jimmy's Bar & Grill to grab a bite. We were both broken hearted over others. We decided to help each other get over them and move on by dating each other! After that, we started having lunch together every day, so rumors started at work. Two weeks later we decided that our dating probably was not a good idea, and we agreed that we should just be friends. We tried to joke about how silly it was for us to be together. We laughed about our list of differences: one of us was a Democrat, the other a Republican; one of us liked dark beer, the other light; etc. (That list was very short and had nothing of significance. Our core values were the same!) We tried to ignore our deep attraction to each other. After a week apart, we were both miserable. We resumed dating on the Q.T.

One night in August we were at Diane's house sitting on the couch next to each other and seriously contemplating our future. Tim looked away, closed his eyes, and looked back and said to Diane, "You are the one." He had closed his eyes and prayed, *"God, give me a sign if she is not the one."* So we had God's blessing—we just had to figure out how to let everyone else know we were even interested in each other.

When Tim asked the man who was not only his boss, but Diane's boss and Diane's father, for his blessing on our marriage, Diane's father gave Tim an assignment to read a book before we got married, Stephen Covey's *"The Seven Habits of Highly Effective People."* Tim did, and it inspired us to write our marriage mission statement. We had it printed on our wedding program and a framed copy still hangs on our bedroom wall.

We have raised two daughters and have tried to instill in them the values of faith, family, and love, which we both hold dear to our hearts—and to marry their best friend.

Secrets for Success: In answer to your question about how to have a successful marriage, we'll share a portion of our marriage mission statement:

"We embrace a life of interdependence. We are each other's partner and best friend. We pledge to love and support each other unconditionally and realize that the success of our marriage lies in our commitment to communicate with each other openly, honestly, and with regard to each other's feelings. We view this marriage as synergistic. It is greater than the both of us and we value the unique qualities that we each bring to this union."

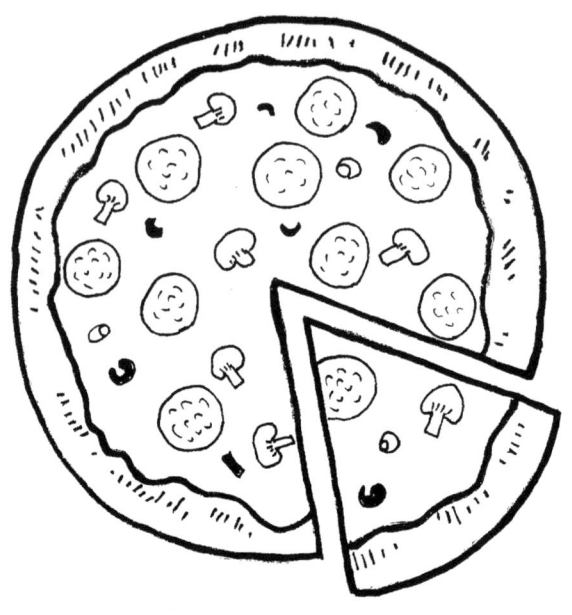

John & Laura, as told by John

One night late in the fall of 1990, when Laura was 19 and I was 20, we were each convinced by our separate, respective groups of high school friends to shelve college and work to enjoy an evening at a popular young adult dance club in Toledo. We later compared stories and knew that neither of us was easy to convince, as we were both pretty conservative individuals who did not party away our time. But this one time our friends prevailed and we ended up at the same dance club that evening. While there, we saw each other for the first time and were immediately drawn to each other. However, every time Laura was away from the friends she came with, there was a young man hanging by her side. I couldn't tell if he was a boyfriend, or just someone being a pest. Either way, the evening went by with no opportunity for us to speak to each other.

The very next evening, both of us showed interest in returning to the same dance club. This really surprised our friends, who had had to coerce and cajole us to get us there the first time. This evening I found Laura and observed that the other young man was not hanging on her every word. Finally, I had a chance to meet her and we had a great conversation. We talked and danced right up to the time we had to depart for the evening. I escorted Laura to her car and we agreed to meet again.

I had an issue to deal with before that meeting could take place. My high school girlfriend had an "on again, off again" relationship with me. At this point we had been off again three or four times. It was pretty clear to me that it was over, however, I wasn't sure she would see it that way. Eventually, I did break the news that this was the final off again time, mainly due to my immediate attraction to Laura when we met.

Laura grew somewhat impatient at the lack of call back from me, not knowing I had this issue to deal with. So Laura grabbed a friend and headed down to Bowling Green. This was very unlike Laura, as she was not the type to pursue a man. But something was different now with me, and she knew it. Laura remembered that I told her that while I was in school for my real estate license, I was working at the local pizza shop delivering pizzas to the college crowd. Laura is tragically bad at directions. Try as she may, she could not find the pizza shop to dine in and casually strike up a conversation with me. Being the resourceful type, she located a pay phone (no cell phones in those days!) and called the pizza shop. You can imagine my surprise when the manager on duty informed me that he had a special request to have the pizza delivered to a red convertible parked in front of the convenience store next door. It did not take me long to figure out I had waited a bit too long to end the other relationship and call Laura. I was very happy for the opportunity to meet again. Laura ordered a simple $3.50 pizza (imagine those prices!) and paid with a $5.00 bill. To this day, I have kept that $5.00 bill in a safe place. I knew this was a special lady and the start of a great relationship.

After more than a year of dating, we became engaged, and we were married in October, 1993. We have been married 20 wonderful years. We've had some very hard times as well. I believe all couples do in the 3 to 6 year range of their marriage. The newness wears off, and the pressures of work and children come along. It requires work on both parts to keep it all together.

Secrets for Success: We thank and praise God for his guidance in our lives. We believe in the saying that "The family who prays together, stays together." I was raised in the Christian faith and Laura was raised Catholic. We had a lot of time to discuss this. We decided during our engagement that we did not want a house divided in faith and that our children would be raised to attend one house of worship each weekend and not skip back and forth between parental beliefs. I investigated the Catholic faith and was able to work through joining the Catholic life prior to our marriage. The Catholic faith may not be for everyone. But one of its teachings is that you think about marriage as the Lord intended of a union between two individuals and God, resembling the Holy Trinity, witnessed by other members of blood and faith families. You pick a faith as a couple, live it every day and include

138

your children in the process. If you do not have a strong faith life, where do you turn when your marriage needs work? We can see the fruits of our labor in working so hard at our marriage. Our three beautiful children are able to know the love of God, the love of their faith community, and the love of both of their parents and sets of grandparents.

A good friend of mine would say, "In this North American culture we have a God hole, and we try to put a lot of things in it other than God by way of possessions, vices, etc. There is only one thing that fills that void, and that is faith."

I hope that you find this story of our meeting entertaining and what we consider the success of our marriage as a small bit of inspiration to stay together for the long haul. We pray for the success of marriage in the world and in your home, that all families may know the love of God and the true peace that comes only through Him.

So How Did They Meet?

By introducing himself or herself   16 couples

Through blind dates, fix-ups, or
introductions by other persons   16 couples

Were in the same school, church,
or neighborhood   12 couples

At place of music and dance   6 couples

At college   5 couples

At work or related to work   5 couples

At a party or social gathering   4 couples

As members of a wedding party   1 couple

In a special interest class   1 couple

(Some couples were included in more than one category above because a part of their "how" was a factor of their "where.")

Invitations

Perhaps you'd like to learn more about asset protection and/or estate, disability and legacy planning to provide for yourself, as well as the ones you love.

Perhaps you would like to learn more about how to include your voice (your story, your essence, your personality) in your plan as part of your legacy to your beneficiaries.

Perhaps you have a plan in place, but it is over five years old, or your circumstances have changed, so it needs a review and tune-up.

Perhaps you just want a second opinion on your current estate plan.

In all cases, if you are an Ohio resident, please consider attending one of our free, monthly seminars at Bayer, Papay & Steiner Co., LPA, Maumee, Ohio, or scheduling a private counseling appointment. Call 419-891-8884 for the seminar schedule and to make reservations, or to make an appointment. If you are not an Ohio resident, please consult the following websites to locate an estate planning attorney licensed in your state:

Wealth Counsel
www.wealthcounsel.com/members-by-zip/

NAELA (National Association of Elder Law Attorneys)
www.naela.org/at the "Find An Attorney" Button

Purposeful Planning Institute
http://purposefulplanninginstitute.com/
(Graduate listing to be added soon.)

141

About Our Law Firm:
Bayer, Papay & Steiner Co., LPA

Debbie J. Papay, Attorney

Debbie J. Papay graduated from Davis College, in Toledo, Ohio in 1975 with an Associate Degree, summa cum laude. Debbie achieved her B.A. in Business Administration and Management from Siena Heights College, summa cum laude in 1981, and her Doctor of Jurisprudence Degree from the University of Toledo, College of Law, magna cum laude in 1985. She began working in law offices in 1974. Since 1985 she has been an attorney concentrating in estate and trust planning and administration, probate, and real estate, and for many years in elder law, Medicaid and the VA Pension. Debbie is licensed to practice law in Ohio and is specially accredited by the Veterans Administration to assist veterans and their surviving spouses in applying for the VA Pension for long term care.

The late baby of a late baby, Debbie was raised with a fondness for "the elders" which has helped shape her practice of law. In 2005 Debbie became the first attorney in northwest Ohio to obtain a Gerontology Certificate from Mercy College. In 2008 she and her law partner, Chris E. Steiner, became the first two area attorneys to be accredited by the Veterans Administration. Since that time Debbie has attended specialized VA Pension and Medicaid training in Boston, New Hartford, Chicago, Atlanta, Dallas and Columbus.

While in law school, Debbie's law review article was published and she served as a Note and Comment

Editor. Since then Debbie has been a contributing author to two hardbound books: *Strictly Business: Planning Strategies for Privately Owned Businesses,* and *Love, Money, Control: Reinventing Estate Planning,* both Quantum Press, LLC, 2002 and 2004. She also wrote *Blooper Episodes in Estate Planning and Elder Law: Lessons From Prime Time TV,* and *Lasting Love...How It's Found: True Tales as Told to Debbie J. Papay, Attorney, Volume I,* Olive Grove Press, LLC, 2012 and 2014.

Debbie has served on the Boards of Directors of the Lutheran Home at Toledo, Planned Pethood, and Davis College, and been an officer and member of several local professional organizations, including Toledo Women's Bar Association, Senior Collaborative, and BNI. Debbie and her husband, Brian Carder, have been married for over 34 years. They make Maumee, Ohio, their home, with Olive, their yellow lab.

Chris E. Steiner, Attorney

Chris E. Steiner attained his Bachelor of Education Degree from the University of Toledo, magna cum laude, in 1974. In 1977, he earned a Doctor of Jurisprudence Degree from its College of Law.

Chris entered the private practice of law in 1978, and became a partner in the law firm of Spengler, Nathanson, Heyman, McCarthy & Durfee in 1984. He worked primarily in the areas of estate planning, business acquisitions and mergers, real estate, and commercial law. After a brief period as a corporate attorney, Chris re-entered the private practice of law in 1986. Chris concentrates his current practice of law in the areas of estate and life planning, charitable giving, special needs planning, business matters, real estate, and elder law, including the VA Pension.

Chris is a contributing author to The *Charitable Giving Handbook*, published by National Underwriter, 1997, and three hardbound books published by Quantum Press: *Strictly Business: Planning Strategies for Privately Owned Businesses*; *Giving: Philanthropy for Everyone*; and *Love, Money, Control: Reinventing Estate Planning* (2002, 2003 and 2004).

For more than 20 years, Chris has served as the attorney for the Maumee Watershed District, formerly the Toledo District of the United Methodist Church. He is a four time delegate from West Ohio to the General and Jurisdictional Conferences of the United Methodist Church.

Chris and his wife, Ann, have been married for over 40 years and have four children: two daughters and two sons. They are the proud grandparents of five wonderful grandchildren. Chris is very active in church and community affairs, and also finds time to water ski, umpire high school baseball and softball games, and referee high school football games. He is also a veteran college football official, having recently retired after 30 years on the college gridiron.

BAYER, PAPAY & STEINER CO., LPA

Counselors & Attorneys at Law

Debbie J. Papay and Chris E. Steiner are the co-owners of their law firm, Bayer, Papay & Steiner Co., LPA, formed between them in 1998 to combine their two law practices with Richard W. Bayer's firm, "Bayer Attorneys." The firm is conveniently located in Maumee's beautiful Arrowhead Park, just off exits from the Ohio Turnpike and Interstates 75 and 475 (US 23), in a one story, accessible building with free, adjacent parking. In keeping with one of their mottos, namely "Educate to Motivate," the attorneys present a free workshop once a month in the law firm's Learning Center on estate planning topics. The attorneys frequently present workshops in outside locations and are available for speaking engagements.

Debbie and Chris are both licensed attorneys in the state of Ohio, as well as VA accredited attorneys authorized to prepare, present, and prosecute claims for the Veterans Pension before the Department of Veterans Affairs.

Bayer, Papay & Steiner Co., LPA or its attorneys are members of Wealth Counsel, LLC; NAELA (National Association of Elder Law Attorneys); LWP (Lawyers With Purpose); the Ohio Forum; the Ohio State, Lucas County and Toledo Bar Associations; Christian Legal Society; and NOGA (Northwest Ohio Gerontological Association). The firm supports the Maumee Chamber of Commerce, as well as a number of other area organizations. Its attorneys attend significant hours of continuing education annually and are in weekly communication with estate planning attorneys around the country on topics affecting their clients.

Debbie and Chris concentrate their combined law practice in all areas of estate planning and administration and elder law, as well as the areas of law that are closely involved with those activities (for example, real estate, business, Medicaid and the VA Pension). With over 4,000 estate planning and trust clients, they are uniquely qualified not just to write estate plans, but to administer them as well. Debbie and Chris encourage a lifelong relationship with their clients, as well as their next generation. They are mindful of their office mottos, "Plans That Work^{SM} By People Who Care," and "Helping Seniors and Those Who Love Them."

Debbie and Chris encourage their clients to pass on some of their personality and their legacy to their heirs when they plan their estates, instead of just willing their wallets. They offer unique tools to do this, known as Purposeful Trusts™. Debbie and Chris are especially pleased to be participants of the Master Program of the Purposeful Planning Institute.

Another advantage they have that differentiates Debbie and Chris from many estate planning attorneys is that in *preparing* plans to be implemented in the *future,* they have the benefit of knowing "how the story turns out." This means that with over six decades of experience between them administering literally hundreds of decedents' Wills and Trusts, written by both them and by other attorneys, they have seen how old plans worked (or didn't) when it actually came time to implement them. This experience is invaluable in the planning and drafting stages for new plans. Debbie and Chris also have access to the collective wisdom and experience of nationwide networks of estate planning attorneys to which they belong. For their clients, this is like having a large team of experienced estate planning attorneys in a back office from which to gain additional insight and planning strategies!

Debbie and Chris devote themselves to the thorough and professional service of clients of all ages who want to plan for their future or need to administer the estate or trust of a loved one.

Bayer, Papay & Steiner Co., LPA
By Appointment Only, 419-891-8884
1925 Indian Wood Circle, Suite A, Maumee, OH 43537
Located in Arrowhead Park, at the corner of
Tomahawk Drive and Indian Wood Circle,
across from the Toledo Area Humane Society.

www.PlansThatWork.net   steiner@PlansThatWork.net
info@PlansThatWork.net   papay@PlansThatWork.net

For educational information about estate planning and elder law, and specific examples of what NOT to do, all presented with humor and nostalgia in the form of Baby Boomer TV show episodes, please consider reading our book, *"Blooper Episodes in Estate Planning and Elder Law: Lessons From Prime Time TV."* Copies are available at www.OliveGrovePress.com or at our law firm (please call ahead).

Appendix—Illustrations

The following illustrations are original drawings by
Brogan L. Carder:

Page 11, Egg Carton
Page 76, Sock Hop

The following illustrations were sketched by others as
inspired by the purchased image listed below:

Pg 1, School house   ©PinkPueblo/Shutterstock.com
Pg 7, 1930's Dancers ©makar/Shutterstock.com
Pg 14, Willow Tree   ©ukmooney/Shutterstock.com
Pg 20, Model A Coupe   ©basel101658/Shutterstock.com
Pg 34, Church   ©Viktoria/Shutterstock.com
Pg 38, Flowerpot   ©bioraven/Shutterstock.com
Pg 38, Garden Tools   ©LHF Graphics/Shutterstock.com
Pg 40, Hot Dog   ©LHF Graphics/Shutterstock.com
Pg 42, Perfume   ©RATOCA/Shutterstock.com
Pg 47, Great Gams   ©Medvedka/Shutterstock.com
Pg 50, Playground   ©igor malovic/Shutterstock.com
Pg 55, Wishbone   ©Tancha/Shutterstock.com
Pg 55, Nail   ©Seamartini Graphics/Shutterstock.com
Pg 57, Football   ©HitToon.com/Shutterstock.com
Pg 60, Fireplace   ©VladisChern/Shutterstock.com
Pg 63, Letter Stack   ©Pixel Embargo/Shutterstock.com
Pg 65, Christmas Tree ©Klara Viskova/Shutterstock.com
Pg 68, Diner Sign   ©Sam72/Shutterstock.com
Pg 70, Three Ribbon   ©Alhovik/Shutterstock.com
Pg 73, Burger & Soda   ©OhnMar/Shutterstock.com
Pg 79, Name Badge   ©vector illustration/Shutterstock.com
Pg 81, Station Attendant ©RetroClipArt/Shutterstock.com
Pg 86, Retro Car Keys ©Ficus777/Shutterstock.com
Pg 88, Airplane   ©Harish Marnad/Shutterstock.com
Pg 91, Lake Canoe   ©LHF Graphics/Shutterstock.com
Pg 93, Typewriter   ©LHF Graphics/Shutterstock.com
Pg 96, Airmail   ©tillydesign/Shutterstock.com

Pg 99, Grocery Bag	©MC Artworks/Shutterstock.com
Pg 99, Carrot Tops	©Oko Laa/Shutterstock.com
Pg 105, Figure Skate	©maximmmmum/Shutterstock.com
Pg 108, Telephone	©grmarc/Shutterstock.com
Pg 113, Paddlewheel Ship	©patrimonio designs ltd/Shutterstock.com
Pg 117, Mail Box	©Martina Vaculikova/Shutterstock.com
Pg 117, Medical Symbol	©mamanamsai/Shutterstock.com
Pg 120, Laundry Line	©Ron and Joe/Shutterstock.com
Pg 123, Michigan-Ohio	©amorfati.art/Shutterstock.com
Pg 127, Martial Arts Diva	©Yu Lan/Shutterstock.com
Pg 132, Stick Figures	©Hannah Ensor/Shutterstock.com
Pg 132, Projector	©DimaGroshev/Shutterstock.com
Pg 132, Clapper Board	©bmnarak/Shutterstock.com
Pg 136, Pizza	©LHF Graphics/Shutterstock.com

Other illustrations were sketched as inspired by personal photos or images in the public domain.